BEISEL

autograph page

Silver Lining

Author: Elizabeth Beisel

Coauthor: Beth Fehr

Contributing Editor: Marla McKenna

Associate Editor: Griffin Mill

Proofreader: Lyda Rose Haerle

Cover Design: Michael King, LoudEdge, Inc.

Interior & Cover Layout: Michael Nicloy

Elizabeth Beisel is represented by:
Cejih Yung, CG Sports Management
www.cgsportsmanagement.com

All photos courtesy of Elizabeth Beisel unless otherwise noted
Front Cover Photo: Chelsey Frost
Back Cover, Autograph Page, and Author Bio Photos:
Kateland Cornine

ISBN: 978-1945907517

Published by
Nico 11 Publishing & Design
Mukwonago, Wisconsin
www.nico11publishing.com

Be well read.

Quantity order requests can be emailed to:
mike@nico11publishing.com

Printed in The United States of America

JTN

For Mom, Dad, and Danny;
for everyone who has made an impact on my life.

FOREWORD

BY GREGG TROY

For almost four decades, I have been associated with some of the greatest people and student athletes through the sport of swimming. As a coach at the age group, high school, collegiate, international, and Olympic level, it has been my good fortune to work with and coach swimmers throughout various points of their athletic pursuits.

The development of work ethic, patience, consistency, time management, dedication, and self-development are all characteristics that are enhanced through a swimming career. The combination of leadership, social skills, and commitment not only enhance athletic performance but also become building blocks for successful life experiences. Using these key assets beyond the athletic career is not accomplished by all—few actually do. Elizabeth Beisel is one of this special group.

I first met Elizabeth when she was 13 at the Pan Pacific Championships. I was blown away by her ability to work hard and race against the best in the world at such a young age. A few years later, she was at a training camp in Colorado with her club coach, Chuck Batchelor. I was coincidentally in Colorado at the same time coaching my Florida athletes. Even at age 15, she was one of the best athletes in the world. Over the course of that week it was obvious to me that she was much more than just that. Elizabeth's demeanor exuded high energy, a big personality, and a vivacious outgoing confidence. She knew no strangers, interacted with all in a confident manner, and feared very little. In short, she was a bubbling cauldron of energy. In a discussion with my wife relative to the possibility of Elizabeth becoming a student athlete at the University of Florida (where I coached), my response was that working with her would be fantastic but "she would be a handful in the best way possible." And let me tell you, I was right. Elizabeth was a handful, but she was also one of the greatest athletes with whom I have ever worked.

Two years after her first Olympics, she stepped onto the University of Florida's campus as a freshman. I ended up working with her for the next eight years. Coaching Elizabeth was a tremendous experience. I had the privilege of watching her develop further as an elite athlete, winning numerous national titles, world titles, and Olympic medals. During this time, she was a fierce competitor, a 4.0 GPA student, and a leader respected by all. Although her training in and out of the water was demanding (30+ hours weekly), coupled with her time-consuming school commitments, Elizabeth managed to carry over all the traits that made her an outstanding athlete to also be a well-rounded individual and a social dynamo. Her passion and hard work took her well beyond her actual athletic talents to levels that few thought she would ever achieve. She made everyone around her a better person, and her positive attitude was infectious.

Elizabeth handled her successes with great humility and pushed herself to aspire to even higher goals. She, in turn, encouraged others to follow. In striving towards her dreams, Elizabeth maintained a fierce commitment and loyalty to her family ties and to her past coaches and friends. Although there were many successes and high points, there were also low points, challenges, and failures. These marked her integrity and grit. In particular, her handling of a disappointing silver medal performance in the 2012 Olympics in London displayed her maturity, resilience, and class, which defined her career. Few athletes have such success at each stage of their career, but even fewer can transfer these experiences to the next chapter.

While still young in the eyes of many, Elizabeth's candid storytelling in this book of her experiences as a young woman maturing through athletics and hardships can serve as both insightful and enjoyable reading that people from all walks of life can relate to and use as a tool for their own success.

A Note From Elizabeth...

Dreams, no matter how big or small, fuel us. They keep us up late at night, push us through our darkest moments of doubt, and remind us why we dedicate ourselves to a journey that might lead to failure. The pursuit of a dream is not for the faint of heart. It takes time, sacrifice, resilience, and perseverance. But let me tell you, when a dream comes true, it is the deepest form of happiness we can experience as humans. I have only experienced this feeling once in my life, and it happened the moment my biggest dream came true.

My first memory of the Olympics was nothing out of the ordinary. In fact, it was probably a carbon copy of what most people experience. It was seven-year-old me, sitting on the couch with my parents, watching swimming during the 2000 Sydney Olympic Games on NBC. Me being a swimmer and knowing that swimming is never broadcasted on television, it was going to take a natural disaster to peel my eyes away from the television.

While watching the best swimmers in the world compete at the pinnacle of their sport, something special happened; it was the first time I truly grasped what the Olympic Games represented, and I knew I had to be there one day. Not to spectate, but to compete. When the allotted hour of swimming was over on NBC, I sprinted to the dial up computer and opened the search engine and typed in "odds of becoming a US Olympic Swimmer." Before my parents could get to the computer to see what I was up to, the search results popped up and revealed the number ".0065%". I turned around to see my parents looking over my shoulder with their jaws to the floor and watched the color drain from their skin. The look of wanting to protect me from such wild aspirations was plastered across both of their faces. Without missing a beat, I stood up and displayed a huge smile on my face and said "Mom...Dad...there's actually a chance!"

Here is the reality. Everyone has a chance. Dreams do not discriminate against their pursuers. But the biggest and wildest dreams come with the greatest risk for failure and disappointment. So, when the search results popped up with that .0065%, all I saw was a chance. But in all fairness, not a great one.

A few months after watching the Sydney Olympic games on television, an Olympic swimmer named Amanda Beard who had competed in those very Olympic games, was hosting a clinic for young swimmers in Boston. It was the talk of the town, and I begged my parents to take me to meet her. My parents agreed and made the trek to Boston on a cold November morning. I sat in the back seat with my swimsuit, cap, and goggles on the entire ride. I was ecstatic. The clinic was held at Harvard University, and I remember thinking it was the most beautiful pool in the entire world. Amanda walked out in her Olympic sweats and had all of us sit down on the bleachers while she stood in front of us and spoke. I was enamored by her. She was brilliant, beautiful, and an Olympic hero. At the end of her motivational speech she looked at the sixty of us and paused. She emphatically and carefully said one sentence, making eye contact with each and every one of us. "At least one of you in this room will be an Olympian one day." I remember hearing that and getting full body chills, knowing it was going to be me. Knowing I was going to be a part of that .0065%. Knowing that one day, I was going to be hosting a clinic like Amanda and inspiring the next generation of Olympic hopefuls. That night when I got home, I wrote one line in my journal that I still have to this day. It simply read "I will be an Olympian one day."

Eight years later in 2008, my dream came true. I became an Olympian, and one of my teammates representing the United States of America that year was Amanda Beard.

Between the time of my clinic with Amanda and my qualifying for the Olympic team, I dedicated my life to the pursuit of my dream. I treated every single day as an opportunity to get better and made the most out of everything. Every single action had a purpose. I said no to things that everyone else was saying yes to. My dream poured over into every crevice of my life, and as crazy as my dream was, I wholeheartedly believed I could do it. I write this now having competed in three Olympic Games and winning two Olympic medals in the process.

For a dream to come true it does not require talent, a certain IQ, specific physical attributes, or any other false prerequisites society might force upon you. A dream come true requires hard work, uncompromising belief in yourself, and a fiery passion towards your pursuit. My dream took eight years to accomplish, and time was always the true test. I never put an expiration date on my dream because I knew I would never stop trying. I believe every single thing we put out into the universe comes back to us at some point. The universe heard all of my dreams and sacrifices, and it responded. Now it's your turn, as the reader, to become inspired and fearless in the pursuit of your own dream. Here's to becoming a part of your own unique .0065%.

From the foreword of the book **Manifesting Your Dreams**.

SILVER LINING

INTRODUCTION

For as long as I can remember, my dream was to go to the Olympics. So, when I walked into my first Olympic Trials at the age of fifteen, it felt surreal to think that I could leave an Olympian. The 2008 Olympic Trials were held in Omaha, Nebraska, at the Qwest Center (now CenturyLink Center), a massive stadium, which seated a sold-out crowd of nearly 15,000 people. I had always imagined that the Olympic Trials would be a large-scale affair, but this event was bigger than I could have ever dreamed possible. The 10-lane 50-meter pool was lined with deck-side flames, which literally shot fire when a world record was set; music pulsed throughout the arena, and spotlights flooded down spiraling from the ceiling. Not only was the roar of the crowd audible, the competitors were seasoned Olympians whose names I knew and strokes I recognized. I was among the best swimmers in the world, on the grandest stage I had ever seen.

Compared to the meets that consisted of heat after heat of swimming in a fluorescently lit pool with polite commentating, this felt like a rock show and we were the stars. I had worked so hard and now here I was, given the greatest platform in the country, and I was ready. I fed off the energy of the crowd and the luminosity of the venue. Not only was this the most amazing setting in which I had ever swum, my events were lined up perfectly. Day one, there was absolutely no pressure. I could enjoy the atmosphere, relax, and soak in the spectacle the Olympic Trials displayed. The only event I had to worry about on that day was the 400 IM (individual medley). I was seeded 12th in the preliminaries, and because only the top two athletes in each event advance to the Olympics, there wasn't any expectation or unnecessary stress. It was my warm-up event, and all I had to do was show up and compete. My main event, the 200 backstroke was a full four days away, so I had time to prepare and bask in the magic of the magnanimous meet.

Considering my place in the rankings going into the 400 IM, I knew I wasn't going to make the finals. I felt lucky just to be able to swim and have the opportunity to test drive the whole experience of the pool, the lights, and the crowd before my big event. I was seeded second in the 200 backstroke, and I knew that if I wanted to make the Olympic team, I had to be on my game. In swimming, hundredths of a second are often the difference between winning and losing, and I wasn't going to let anything get in my way of qualifying for the Beijing Olympic Games. Having a low-key event the first day was ideal.

I wasn't nervous at all before the 400 IM preliminaries. The invigoration from the cheers produced by the crowd energized me, and I ate up every second of the lights, the music, and the intensity of the meet. I loved the attention of the spectators and having the honor of standing on the pool deck with swimmers who I had watched throughout my career. Warm-ups were uneventful, and before long, I found myself waiting to be announced to take my place on the block. You have around three minutes once the swimmers are announced until the race starts, and I'd argue that those three minutes are what separate good swimmers from great swimmers. In order to be great, all sports require one thing—an ability to thrive under pressure. If you can't take the heat and put up the performance when it counts, all of the training, practices, and hours logged don't matter. If you want to win, you have to show up when the stakes are high.

Looking back now, I didn't know that yet. All I knew was that I wasn't intimidated by the number of people, the theatrical grandeur of the rock star vibe, or the presence of swimmers who had already made a name for themselves. I loved it. Standing in the darkness as my name was announced, I wasn't afraid. I couldn't wait to dive off of that block for my first event and leave everything I had in the pool. I shook out my arms as music blasted, and I heard screams coming from the audience, who I couldn't see because I was blinded by the spotlight which washed over me. This wasn't how I had imagined the Olympic Trials would be—it was eons better. I had never felt more alive than standing on that block, surrounded by the crowd, and about to swim in front of thousands. It didn't matter that the 400 IM wasn't my event. I was going to pay attention to the start and the dynamics of each stroke I took and every single turn. When all was said and done, even though this wasn't the event that was going to get me to the Olympics, I would give it my absolute all. The only thing I concentrated on was doing my best.

Once all of the swimmers stood on the pool deck, it was just like any other race. Except it wasn't. I couldn't get the flaming poolside spurts out of my mind or shut out the thunderous roar that came from the stands. Everything felt different, and my body was ignited in a way I had never experienced before. When we took our marks on the blocks, I could barely contain the explosive energy that boiled within. Once I heard the starting beep, I flew off the block and into the water. My strokes had never felt smoother, and I moved through the pool with fluidity that I had worked hard to master. All of the practices, all of the hours, all of the times I had woken up early or stayed late at practice, somehow in that moment everything came together. A 400 IM takes speed, but it also requires a significant amount of endurance, and even I was surprised with the pace I was able to maintain up until the very end. Once I hit the wall, I was elated. I immediately glanced up at the scoreboard that sat above the pool. I was sure that I had easily beat my own best time, but when I saw my name and flames roaring their way towards the ceiling, my heart began to thud even faster in my chest.

I tried to catch my breath as the sounds from the crowd became louder. Something was wrong. This wasn't how I had foreseen the trials going. The 400 IM wasn't my event, I was a backstroker. I tried to process what was happening, but it didn't seem real. I waited for it to hit me, for everything to become more visceral, but as I read my time, I felt my stomach churn. I had just broken the Olympic Trials record in the 400 IM at 15 years old, and the pressure of the world was on me.

CHAPTER ONE

Growing up in the Ocean State of Rhode Island, I've always had a deep love and appreciation for the water. Whether it be the breathtaking beaches where I grew up, the pool in my backyard, or diving off a block in an Olympic stadium; water is always where I've felt most at home. Even as a baby, the only way my mother could calm me was during bath time or by running warm water over my thick head of hair in the sink.

As an infant, I was so difficult that my entire family referred to me as "The Fuss." Not only was I inconsolable any time I was out of the water, but when my parents put me to bed with a bottle, the second I was finished I would chuck it so hard that marks lined the wall near my crib. I had an enormous amount of energy and almost never slept. So my mother was beyond relieved when I finally turned six months old, and she was able to enroll me in "Mommy and Me" swim classes at the local YMCA. That was when everything changed.

My parents had a hunch that I may be a "water baby," and they couldn't have been more right. Most of the infants screamed throughout the duration of the class, thrashing their arms and working themselves into a frenzy. I entered the water giggling, with a wide smile, and loved every moment. My mother was ecstatic. At "Mommy and Me" classes, she finally got a 30-minute break from my incessant tantrums and savored the time we spent together at the pool. The instructor took notice of my ease and joy in the water and told my mom that she could bring me in more than the prescribed once a week class. By the end of that first month, I was in the water five times a week. Soon my days as "The Fuss" were nothing but a distant memory, my volatile moods seemingly cured.

For the next five years, I spent almost every day in the water. The Little Mermaid was my favorite Disney princess, and one of the happiest moments of my childhood was when I turned five and got a monofin, which allowed me to flit about the pool as if I was an actual mermaid. Whether it was the YMCA, our backyard pool, or my grandparents' beach house in Bonnet Shores, if my parents wanted me to sleep through the night, I had to have my daily dose of water.

Needless to say, contrary to the popular stereotype of parents who pressure their young children into intense athletics, my parents never pushed swimming on me. Being in the water was something I innately loved and intensely craved, and the only activity that could harness my boundless energy. At five years old, I was the one begging them to let me join a swim team. My mother agreed and took me to tryouts at the YMCA where I had first learned to swim. I was so excited. The thought of being able to swim every single day in the big kid pool was literally a dream come true. I had my suit, my cap, and even my goggles on before we had left the house. However, my mother was sternly told that no children under six would be allowed to tryout. The head coach even recommended that because of my small size, gymnastics may be a better fit. I was devastated.

I sobbed the entire drive home. I couldn't wrap my head around why they wouldn't let me join the swim team. For an entire week I did nothing but sulk and adamantly refused to get in the water. When my parents tried to be encouraging and suggested that I might like gymnastics, I was outraged. "I hate gymnastics!" I screamed. Of course, at that age I didn't know what gymnastics was, but all that mattered was it wasn't swimming. The only other activity I enjoyed was playing the violin, which I did for hours in my room. But no matter how much time I spent making music, the void that only water could fill remained. My parents searched for other local swim teams, but received the same response. I was too young and too small to even tryout. This rejection and disappointment only added to my explosive temperament and my parents had no idea what to do. My brother, Danny, who was a year younger, had the same amount of energy and gusto I did. As youngsters, we were nearly impossible to tie down; we were in all places at all times. And it would be a major understatement to say that my parents really had their hands full. After a few weeks they decided they had to try something and had a brilliant idea—diving.

Diving involved components of gymnastics but the sport also included my favorite element, water. Luckily, the diving team allowed children of all ages and sizes to join, and just three months after I turned five, my parents drove me to the University of Rhode Island where I was able to try out for the team. The main criteria for children that young was that you could jump off of a one-meter board and competently swim to the wall. After that day, I was in. My parents were thrilled when I was given the green light to join the Rams Diving Club.

Practice was only twice a week, which was nowhere close to being enough to satisfy me. But after the swim team rejections my parents were just grateful I had the opportunity to be a part of the team. Diving served as an interim before I was officially allowed to swim. I never excelled at the sport, and the only part I liked was when I got to catapult into the deep end. Some of the other children were elegant, with pointed toes and clean entries. My goal was to make the biggest splash possible, which wasn't exactly what my coach wanted. But I didn't care. I had my eye on the older kids on the swim team who practiced at the same time we did. On the way home from the pool, I would incessantly ask my mom and dad if I could try out for the swim team the next week. My parents knew just as well as I did that the moment I turned six, diving would be a thing of the past.

Finally, after much anticipation, my sixth birthday arrived. I was still much smaller than most swimmers my age, so even once I hit the six-year mark the head coach was reluctant to allow me to join. Thankfully, my parents weren't taking no for an answer. They knew how much I loved swimming and that getting on the team meant the world to me. My mom and dad wanted me to have fun and be able to burn off some of my insatiable energy. The extent of my parents' swimming experience was that my mom used to lifeguard at the local beaches during the summers when she was a teenager. So, when I was finally accepted as a member of the Rams Swimming Club which practiced at the University of Rhode Island, the only goal was participation. My parents were overjoyed not to have to hear me complain about not being able to swim on a team, and I quickly found my place as a Ram.

The regular swimming helped me funnel my energy productively, and I quickly settled into a routine with the Rams. My parents were tremendously relieved once I found this outlet, and from then on, our household was relatively normal. Danny and I both had rambunctious streaks, but with sports we were able to channel that in a positive way. Like most siblings, we had our share of arguments, but we were always close. Both of my parents worked. My mother, Joan, was a compliance agent for American Airlines at the Providence airport. Growing up in Rhode Island, she had spent summers in Bonnet Shores at the beach and attended school in Providence during the rest of the year. My father, Ted, was a construction superintendent. He was born in Green Bay, Wisconsin. My great uncle, Andrew Turnbull, was the first president of the Green Bay Packers. So despite that my father's family eventually moved to New York where he was raised, he's still the biggest Green Bay Packers fan ever—a trait which Danny also inherited. My father met my mother at a bar in New York, they fell in love, and eventually decided to settle in southern Rhode Island, where my mother had loved spending summers when she was young.

Growing up, we lived two blocks away from the beach. My favorite time of year was the summer, when we would make the hot trek to the shoreline on a daily basis. After returning home salty, sandy, and exhausted from spending hours upon hours at the beach, we would rinse off and relax in the pool. Dad would throw fresh seafood on the grill for dinner, and we would eat together outside on our back porch. Our home was always filled with love, laughter, and of course, lots of animals. We had two goats, two pigs, two dogs, one cat, two rabbits, six birds, and two guinea pigs. Danny once had a homework assignment that required him to count the number of legs on our pets at home. The teacher was so bewildered by his answer that she called our house to make sure that my brother, in fact, knew how to count. As Danny and I got more involved in our respective sports, my parents would shuttle us to and from our practices as necessary, and swimming with the Rams became a natural and important part of my life.

I immediately connected with my first coach, Josh LaPlante. When I met him he was in his mid-twenties and had kind dark eyes and dark brown hair. He was personable, charismatic, and I trusted him instantly. At the time, I didn't realize how crucial nailing the fundamentals of swimming would prove to be. Josh made everything fun and straightforward, and even when he was critiquing my stroke or teaching me a new skill he did so with incredible patience and sincere encouragement. Josh was the person who laid the foundation for the rest of my swimming career. He taught me the most efficient techniques for starts and turns and helped me do all of the stroke work that would set me up for success later on.

We practiced five times a week, and depending on the time of year, had swim meets on the weekends. Practice was easily my favorite time of day, and I was grateful to finally be an official member of the Rams. Laura Sogar was one of my first good friends on the team, and I always looked forward to seeing her at the pool. She was a talented swimmer, and she loved animals and Harry Potter just like I did. We got along well and always supported one another at practice as well as outside of the pool. We both were willing to work hard in order to improve and constantly challenged ourselves. As we became more comfortable with the various strokes and events, we started to discover that we both had different strengths. Laura excelled in breaststroke and butterfly, while my best events were backstroke and the individual medley (a combination of all four strokes: butterfly, backstroke, breaststroke, and freestyle, which is referred to in swimming as an IM, for short).

Every practice, I gave it my all. Josh was always there, cheering me on and helping me make corrections so that my strokes, turns, and starts were as dynamic as possible. And then something clicked. I started to get fast, really fast. Swimming was always fun, but I was competitive by nature, and eventually being in the pool wasn't enough. Once I started winning races, I became even more motivated. Not only did I want to win in competition, but I became fixated on beating my own best times. Winning a race was great but if I felt I could get faster, I only pushed myself that much harder. Swimming is divided into age groups, and the eight-and-under group is the youngest designation. By the time I was seven years old, I was one of the fastest swimmers in the country in almost every event in the eight-and-under age group.

Having my hard work and all of the hours of practice at the pool with Josh payoff was rewarding, but I wasn't sure what my future in swimming looked like. Then one evening my parents flipped on the television, and my eyes were glued to the screen. It was coverage from the 2000 Olympics in Sydney. I watched in amazement as the most talented athletes in the world proudly marched in the opening ceremony, their brightly colored outfits honoring their home countries, and their sense of confidence and poise pronounced as they entered the enormous stadium. There was inspirational music, flashing lights, enormous orange and yellow flames, endless fireworks, and those symbolic five interlaced rings were everywhere. Not only had these athletes trained incredibly hard to become the very best, they were now given the opportunity to showcase their talents on the most colossal stage I could imagine. Every chance I got, I watched in awe as the competition in Sydney unfolded, absolutely captivated by the enormity of the Olympic Games.

I had thought about it a lot, and one day as I bounded into practice, ready to jump in the water, I looked up at Josh. I wasn't sure what he would say if I admitted that I had been watching the Sydney Games and that I wholeheartedly wanted to go to the Olympics. But I still remember exactly what he said when I told him. Without missing a beat he gave me a reassuring smile. "If you dream big and work hard, you can do it." He didn't doubt me for a second. At seven years old, having my coach believe that I could make it to the Olympics was all I needed to know that this was a real possibility. To this day, I credit Josh with providing me with all of the basics required to be successful in swimming, including a confidence in my own ability. Had Josh not believed in me, I don't know if I would have believed in myself. But he did and having a coach who steadfastly stood behind me and my dreams made me think that I could take on the world.

Some of the swimmers on my team could put up awesome times in practice, but when it came to competitions, they would buckle under pressure. When I first started competing, I was the opposite. Polishing my strokes and doing speed work with Josh and the other Rams at the pool where I had come to feel at home brought me a great amount of satisfaction. But I relished the opportunity to display my skills on a larger scale than just making the intervals at practice. I loved hearing the crowd cheer as I took my mark on the block before a race, and how adrenaline surged through every part of my body once the high-pitched beep signaled us to start. I would plow through the water as quickly and efficiently as possible, often doing better than even my best practice times, and I generally touched the wall first. That was the best feeling in the world. But even at seven, I knew that our local meets in Rhode Island and Massachusetts were a far cry from the magnitude of the platform that I had watched the athletes compete on in Sydney.

My first real test came at the 1999 Eastern Zones Championships in New Jersey, when I was still just seven years old. This was my first meet that was outside of Rhode Island or Massachusetts, and Laura and I couldn't wait to compete. The entire bus ride we read our Harry Potter books and talked endlessly about what we might find when we arrived. When the bus pulled up to the pool venue, the size of the building alone was daunting.

I'll never forget walking onto the deck of that pool. The crowd there dwarfed the audience at any swim meet I had ever competed in. There were easily hundreds of people in the stands, and the rumble of their applause echoed from the walls. Despite that I was only seven, something in my gut told me that this was a make or break moment. I could see some of my teammates noticeably recoil with the massive amount of noise and the sheer number of people, but the stimulation ran through my veins like fire. It gave me a crackling surge of energy that charged throughout my whole body. I wasn't nervous, and I didn't shy away from the pressure. I couldn't wait to get up on that block and show everyone what I could do. I was a swimmer, that much I knew, and now I had the opportunity to prove it in front of a crowd of hundreds. I was beside myself with excitement. This was my moment, and I was going to give it everything I had.

My best event was the 100 IM, and I knew that I was close to breaking the eight-and-under national age group record, which was held by Olympic champion, Lea Loveless (now Lea Maurer). Lea had medaled at the 1992 Olympics in Barcelona, Spain, and she was someone who I considered a hero. She had done what I wanted to do; go to the Olympics and win gold. So, it was hard for me to believe that I had a shot at breaking a record she had set years prior. But numbers don't lie. I'd have to swim the best time I had ever put up in that event, but I was so close that realistically speaking, breaking her record wasn't an impossibility.

We warmed up as usual, but everything seemed to matter just a little bit more. The competition was fierce, the swimmers and coaches on deck were more serious, and I knew that up until that point, this was the biggest meet of my life. As I waited for my race to begin, I thought about all of the pointers Josh had given me and let myself enjoy the energy of the crowd. It felt like forever, but finally it was my turn. I stood beside the block ready to swim the 100 IM. I stretched my arms, shook out my legs, and took in a deep breath. As I stepped onto the block, the crowd cheered and I stared down at the water. We took our marks, and within an instant, we were off. I had practiced the 100 IM so many times that muscle memory took over, and I used the crowd as an incentive to kick just a little faster and pull just a little bit harder than I ever had before. I could hear cheering from the stands, and with each stroke I got stronger. By the time I reached my last lap, which was freestyle, I knew that it would be close. My strokes felt clean and powerful, and I gave it everything I had until my hand finally hit the wall.

The second I touched, the crowd screamed even louder. I turned to look at the scoreboard where our times were instantaneously posted. I couldn't believe it. I had just beat Lea Loveless's record, and I could feel my chest swell with pride as the people in the stands continued to applaud. It wasn't the first time I had broken a national age group record, but it was the first time I had done it at a major meet. That meant something, and even at seven years old I knew that. I was proud of myself. I had swum my fastest time when it mattered most. At that moment, I was the best that had ever been in that event. The rest of the meet, those words kept repeating themselves in my mind. The best that had ever been.

CHAPTER TWO

After Zones, I was convinced that Josh was right. If I could break Lea Loveless's record, I could follow in her footsteps. I knew that it would take a lot of hard work, dedication, and commitment, but if I continued down the path I was on, making an Olympic team was more than just a naive dream. I was already one of the fastest swimmers in the country for my age; all I had to do was keep training. Before Zones, I had been serious about my love for swimming, but after that meet, I wanted to do more than just win. I wanted to be the very best.

I had mastered the fundamentals of all of the strokes and the events, but now it was time to fine-tune my skills. There are four strokes in swimming; butterfly, backstroke, breaststroke, and freestyle. I always excelled in the long axis strokes, which are backstroke and freestyle. There was something about those strokes that just clicked—they felt natural and I automatically fell into an easy rhythm. Butterfly and breaststroke, the short axis strokes, were a completely different story. My butterfly wasn't terrible, and Josh had adopted the strategy of "fake it till you make it" when it came to me swimming butterfly. The technique wasn't there and it wasn't as organic as my freestyle and backstroke, but at least I was fast. Breaststroke, on the other hand, was terrible. My timing was consistently off and the stroke made absolutely no sense to me. When it comes to swimming, I think breaststrokers are by far the most talented. Breaststroke takes finesse, patience, and meticulous timing. I had none of these qualities. My instinct was to blindly swim as fast as humanly possible with quick erratic movements, which is a recipe for disaster when it comes to breaststroke. This was particularly frustrating because I had no choice but to swim breaststroke since my best event was the IM. Even with three strong strokes (butterfly, backstroke, and freestyle) I still needed to swim decent breaststroke relatively fast if I ever wanted to be a serious competitor in the event. When I came home from Zones, Josh sat down with me and explained that although my strokes were respectable and I had great speed, we needed to modify my technique if I wanted to improve my times.

Josh already had a plan, and I enthusiastically took on the challenge. However, I quickly found that tweaking the technicality of my strokes was harder than I had expected. Every single week, we would focus on a new stroke during practice. The first week was butterfly. Although butterfly wasn't my worst stroke when it came to speed, it was by far my least favorite. I would argue that according to most swimmers (myself included) butterfly is the most difficult of the four strokes. The physical exertion butterfly demands is intense and the stroke requires a well-developed technique, strong shoulder muscles, and an enormous amount of endurance. By the end of day one, my shoulders and upper body burned with every movement. But I didn't stop. The entirety of that week, every single set and drill I did was butterfly, and when practice was over, merely lifting my arms to pull my wildly curly hair into a ponytail was painful. We worked comprehensively on where I positioned my hands to pull water, the timing of my kick, and the manner in which I breathed. Josh broke the stroke down into sections, dissecting each and every part of the way I swam until I got it right. The following week was backstroke. Even though this was my best stroke, I still had an immense amount of work to do. In swimming, you can only make it so far in the sport with average technique. The greatest swimmers in the world aren't just fast, but incredibly efficient and diligent as well. Josh and I worked on my rotation, making sure that I was entering each hand at the perfect position to grab the most water. We worked on my kick to the point that my legs felt like they would fall off. I spent hours that week working on swimming with a still head, so that my body would stay in a straight line from wall-to-wall. After two weeks of mindful, painstakingly detailed, technique-oriented practices, I was exhausted.

Josh laughed when I walked into practice for the start of week three of stroke work. Week three was breaststroke week and before I even got in the water, I was already miserable. I sulked on the pool deck, dreading trying to tackle the one stroke that I didn't understand. I knew I had to do it, but I wasn't sure I could force myself to get into the pool. Josh gave me a knowing smile, but when he knelt down beside me, the expression on his face turned serious. "Elizabeth, not everyone has a chance to swim on a team like you do. Not everyone has a gift like you do. This week, you have an opportunity to get better. You can check your attitude at the door and work on breaststroke for the next seven days, or you can turn around and come back next week for freestyle." He crossed his arms when I didn't respond. "Don't expect to be the best if you aren't willing to work on your weaknesses. Weaknesses are what keep us going, because weaknesses are the only way we improve."

Even as an eight-year-old, I knew Josh was right. I spent that entire week working on breaststroke, more focused than I had ever been. We picked apart every single element of my stroke—the kick, the pull, my head position, the way I breathed, and put it all back together at the end of practice every day. We would end each practice with two fifty-yard swims; one smooth and focused on technique, and the other fast, working on technique but also incorporating speed. From day one to day seven, I dropped four full seconds on the fast 50, which is unheard of in the world of swimming. It was my first real taste of significant improvement. I had followed Josh's instructions, worked with intention, and it had paid off. In a matter of just one week, I had completely revamped my breaststroke and had become noticeably faster. I got giddy with the thought of what could happen if I spent every single week working that hard and that focused. Maybe I could be the best in the world.

But swimming wasn't the only thing in my life that was ramping up. I still wrestled with wrangling in my seemingly endless supply of energy. I wasn't just passionate about swimming, I wanted to see, do, and try everything. I begged my parents to sign me up for ballet, basketball, piano lessons, and at age eight, I made the transition from regular violin lessons to a more advanced instructor. All of this was on top of school. My parents never said no when I wanted to try something new, and they took on the task of making sure that I made it to all of my activities. They both worked full-time jobs and spent their free hours shuttling Danny and me to practices or lessons. On Wednesdays, my mom would pick me up straight from school with a snack, and I would go to piano, ballet, and swim practice back-to-back-to-back before returning home to eat dinner and start my homework. On Fridays, I went directly from school to violin and then to swim practice. My schedule was jam packed, but growing up, I felt like my life was also balanced. I was focused and committed to lots of activities that I enjoyed instead of being focused solely on swimming.

However, even though I loved lots of things, swimming and violin were inarguably where I shined the brightest. As my times at swim practice continued to get faster, Josh made the decision that twice a week I would practice with the older swimmers. Despite that I was only eight, I could make the intervals the 13-, 14-, and 15-year-old swimmers were doing. I hated that part. I was intimidated because everyone was so much bigger and older, and no one was welcoming to me. I felt left out constantly and spent the whole practice staying as quiet as possible to avoid annoying anyone. One day when I was practicing with the older group, Josh decided to have us do as many fifties as possible while continually taking five seconds off of each interval. If you missed an interval, you were out and had to cheer on the rest of the swimmers that were still in the set. One of the older boys was ahead of me for most of the set, but in the end, I surprisingly beat him. Instead of congratulating me or even ignoring me, he slammed the wall with his fist as hard as he could and screamed my name along with every obscenity I had ever heard. He wasn't angry with himself, at least it didn't seem that way to me. It felt like all of that yelling was directed towards me, and he instantly made me feel ashamed that I had beaten him. After practice, I sprinted to the locker room, changed as fast as I could, and cried the whole way home. Like most young kids, I desperately wanted people to like me, especially the older swimmers. Over the next few weeks, Josh saw that I started holding back at practice and pulled me aside. "What's going on?"

I looked down at the ground. "Nothing."

"I know you can swim better times than you've been doing. Talk to me."

"The older boys get mad when I beat them," I replied. "They hate swimming with me."

Josh knelt down beside me. "That's the thing about being the best. Sometimes it's harder than it looks. But you can't control other people. If you want to get better, you can't let what a bunch of stinky boys think get in your way. When you start winning there's always going to be people who want to beat you. That's the way it works. Instead of worrying about what people think, focus on your swimming. Alright?"

I nodded, jumped back in and did my best to ignore the boys and concentrate on my strokes.

Being skilled at violin was easier. By nature the setup was far less competitive, and I didn't have to practice with anyone older or bigger to get better. Every year in Rhode Island I attended Solo and Ensemble. This is an event where you have the opportunity to play in front of a panel of judges and get graded on technique, tone, accuracy, and other various components of playing the violin. I always received the highest score possible and was consistently rated the "best performance" of my age group. I was just as proud of my musical skills as I was my swimming, and I worked just as hard to accomplish my goals and improve on the violin. The great thing about violin was that it was just me and my instrument. No one got mad at me when I beat them, and I never felt alone or ostracized like I did in the older swimming group. Violin became an escape for me.

Right after my tenth birthday, Sports Illustrated reached out to me because they were doing a story on "The American Athlete: Age 10." The magazine featured five different athletes for the issue, and I was thrilled to participate. I anxiously awaited their questions, but there was one I didn't expect. "Would you rather go to the Olympics in swimming or play in the Boston Pops?" the interviewer asked. I was perplexed. Swimming and playing the violin were intrinsic; they filled me with joy and made me come alive in a way that nothing else could. The pool was where I belonged, but I felt that same sense of completion with a violin on my shoulder. Both playing music and making faster intervals made me happy but in very different and non-comparable ways. The question of one versus the other was never something I had considered. I concentrated hard, trying to decide if I could only go to the Olympics or play for the renowned orchestra—which would I choose? But no matter how much thought I gave to the scenario, I found myself unable to come up with an answer. I loved swimming and the violin equally, and in the end I said that I didn't know. I wanted so badly to do both and it seemed like an impossible hypothetical. I was talented at swimming and the violin, so I saw no reason why I couldn't continue to excel in each if I continued to work hard. And I did.

I maintained my sometimes ridiculously hectic schedule without giving up any of my activities and was able to still do well in school. My parents were beyond supportive and encouraging, constantly driving me to practice after practice, and making sure that I had everything I needed in order to succeed. Although I did enjoy ballet, basketball, and piano, swimming and violin continued to be my greatest loves, and every day I was becoming a faster swimmer and a more skilled violinist. Being busy was how I thrived, and working hard gave me a great sense of achievement.

When I was 10, at the end of the year, we headed to our championship meet at Harvard University. It had been a fantastic season, and I went into the meet feeling confident and excited. I had never grown to like practicing with the older kids, and being so much younger, I still hadn't learned to relate to them. No one ever went out of their way to acknowledge my presence, but I knew that if I wanted to improve, I had to practice with faster swimmers. Often times, Josh was the only person I exchanged words with, and I appreciated the few sentences we spoke to each other more than he ever knew. I had gotten used to going into practice, keeping my head down, and focusing on swimming to the best of my ability, just like Josh said. Even though it wasn't the warm and friendly environment I enjoyed with the Rams my own age, those practices made me a much faster and more competent competitor. When I arrived at Harvard, I couldn't have felt better about my swimming.

I loved competing and racing, and I always looked forward to spending time with the swimmers my own age and cheering on my teammates at meets. It was such a fun atmosphere, and I basked in the limelight when the crowd watched, and as was becoming expected, I hit the wall first. Swim meets, when I was first competing for the Rams, are some of my fondest memories. The expectations were minimal; I was still progressing at an impressive rate, and beating my own best times was always a thrill. I lived for those competitions, and I had never imagined any of it coming to an end. So once Championships were over, when Josh called us all in for a huddle, I immediately ran towards him and sandwiched myself in between my teammates who surrounded him. Everyone had finished their races, and I was excited to hear what he was about to say before making the drive back to Rhode Island with my mom.

As Josh tried to get all of our attention, he forced a smile, but something seemed off. He gave us the usual post meet speech about how proud of us he was and how well we had done. But he lacked his usual zest, and his animated words seemed quieter. His usual charisma was replaced with an eerie sense of reverence. "You all did so well, and it has been such an incredible journey working with each and every one of you," he said sincerely. "But I wanted to let you know that I will not be returning to Rams to coach next year." The second those words fell from his mouth a knot formed in my stomach. I didn't understand. "I wish you all the very best of luck," he continued, but I was no longer listening. I couldn't believe what I had just heard. Josh, my Josh, was leaving?

I couldn't concentrate on anything; my stomach hurt, and my head was spinning. I wanted to throw up, start screaming hysterically, and cry simultaneously, but instead I stared blankly ahead. I didn't say a word and when he was finished, I silently gathered my things, and walked to the car with my mom. Once the doors were closed, tears streamed down my cheeks, and there was nothing she could say or do to console me. When it came to swimming, Josh was my everything. He had been there since day one, and he was the only coach I had ever known. Even when I had to swim with the older kids, he made me feel as if I belonged, which I so intensely craved. I was my very best with Josh. He knew how to challenge me and push me to my threshold without ever compromising my love for the sport. Throughout my entire swimming career, he was the one who had been there, giving me advice, critiques, and he had become more than a coach, he was a mentor and I thought the entire world of him. Josh literally had taken my strokes apart and rebuilt them, and he had always found a way to make me believe in myself. As a 10-year-old, I wasn't aware of the transitory nature of coaching. I had assumed that Josh would be my coach forever. After all, it worked so well and we were such a good team. When we had arrived at Harvard everything was exactly as it should be, but now my 10-year-old reality had been blown to bits.

On that car ride home and in the days that would follow, I questioned everything about swimming. I couldn't picture going to the pool without Josh there, and I wasn't sure that I even wanted to. There were suddenly so many unknowns where certainties had previously existed. If I wasn't going to be coached by Josh, who would I swim for? Was there a future in the sport for me without him? How could I possibly go to practice with the older kids now? Josh had made me believe that anything was possible, but without his presence that conviction was harder to swallow. I felt like the wind had been knocked out of me. The future I had imagined was gone, and I had no idea what would replace the vision I had of Josh coaching me to the Olympics. I didn't know what the rest of my swimming career would look like, but I did know that I wouldn't go back to training at that pool without him.

The end of the year awards ceremony for our team was usually a light and fun event that everyone eagerly anticipated. But that year, it felt like I was attending a funeral. I didn't care if I got an award, and the corny jokes and funny themes weren't enough to make me smile or forget that this marked an end for me. All I wanted to do was to hit the rewind button, go back in time, and make Josh my coach again.

After the festivities, food, awards, and trying to keep a fake smile plastered across my face, I went to find my parents so that we could go home. I searched the room but before I could find my mom and dad, I heard a familiar voice. "Elizabeth!"

I turned to see Josh. He was dressed much more formally than at practice, but his kind eyes and reassuring smile were still the same. I lit up immediately. "Hi Josh!"

Nodding hello, he gestured for me to follow him, which I did. We stood next to the wall, just a few feet from everyone else, and I hoped beyond hope that he was about to tell me that he was coming back. Instead he took a white envelope from his pocket and handed it to me. "This is for you. Open it when you get home, okay?"

As always, I listened to him intently. "Okay. I will."

"Elizabeth, I want you to know that you're an incredible athlete. It has been such an honor to work with you," he paused for a moment.

"You've got more potential than you realize. I can't wait to see what you accomplish in swimming. Don't ever let anyone make you feel like you don't belong. I know that you're going to do great things."

I don't remember what I said in return, but it meant everything to me to hear those words. I held the small white envelope he had handed me as if it was a coveted treasure, and the second I got home I rushed up to my bedroom and carefully opened it. Inside was a glossy card with a picture of blue water, orange lane lines, and a seasoned swimmer mid-stroke, with a quote in capital white letters. "The difference between ordinary and extraordinary is that little extra."

I smiled. That sounded just like something Josh would say to me when I was having a bad day at practice. I opened the card and saw Josh's handwriting inside. He congratulated me on my relay titles, my New England records, and made it clear he believed I was destined for big things. "You are a talented, hardworking, goal-oriented swimmer, and a team leader (great combination)," he continued. Then he gave me one last piece of advice. "Set your goals high enough to be almost unrealistic and you will be amazed at what is possible." At the bottom of the card, he wished me good luck, then signed and underlined his name. I stared at that card for a long time and took his words to heart. I was going to do great things, just like he said. I wasn't sure how or what that road looked like, but I knew I had to keep swimming.

I never saw Josh again after that night, and I've often wondered if he has any idea what an extraordinary impact he made on my life. To this day, there's no doubt in my mind that without Josh, I never would have become the swimmer, the Olympian, or the person I am today. He taught me everything I needed to know about the foundations of swimming, hard work, and persevering through the difficult stuff in order to make your goals a reality. Sixteen years later that card still sits on a shelf in my bedroom and remains one of my most prized possessions.

CHAPTER THREE

The month of August was a difficult one for my family and me. After Josh left, I thought my swimming career was over. But even once I decided that I would continue swimming, the pathway forward remained unclear. The only team of my caliber in the state of Rhode Island was the Rams, and I remained resolute in my decision not to return. There was no way I was going back there to swim without Josh. That left my family and I without a clear alternative. Essentially, we had two choices. I could join Bluefish, the most dominant team in New England, with an amazing reputation but based in Attleboro, Massachusetts—a 45-minute drive one-way; or we could move. Neither choice offered the convenience we had taken for granted when I swam with the Rams, and it wasn't an easy decision.

I didn't swim at all that month. Instead I found release in surfing and playing the violin. Surfing at the beaches nearby gave me the water fix I needed, and playing the violin every single day gave me a sense of peace when everything seemed uncertain. During that time, I was grateful I had the violin to lean into. With my first violin teacher, I was taught using the Suzuki method. The Suzuki method is a very common way to teach young children to play the violin. There are multiple books filled with fairly common pieces that you would find within any basic classical violinist's repertoire. Once I graduated from the Suzuki method and moved on to a more advanced teacher, I started playing much more difficult concertos and sonatas, which required a lot more practice. My teacher, Mr. Dempsey, absolutely loved having me as a student during the month of August that year, and I was happy to have a surplus of time to spend with him. Mr. Dempsey nicknamed me "Vivace" (which is my favorite tempo to play in) from my very first lesson with him. I don't think he ever referred to me by my real name and for some reason that made even the most technical lessons seem lighter and more relaxed. With no scheduled swim practices, I had more time to dedicate to the violin. Which meant Mr. Dempsey could really push me during those four weeks. He helped me use my break from the pool to capitalize on making headway as a violinist. I was able to focus solely on music and Mr. Dempsey always told me that I could make violin a successful career if I truly committed to it.

Even though Mr. Dempsey was "team violin," he understood that swimming was becoming just a little bit higher on my list of priorities, and he never tried to persuade me otherwise. But when I was ready to focus on the violin, he was always there to help me improve. That August, Mr. Dempsey introduced me to some of the most challenging pieces I had ever seen. There were so many notes on a page that they all seemed to blur together, and the music I was playing went from three and four pages, to five and six. I was overwhelmed, but equally excited to broaden my range. I met with him twice a week for an hour and he would work with me on fingering, bowing, and perfecting each part of my technique, just as Josh had done with my strokes in swimming. Soon, I was playing extraordinarily complicated pieces by Saint-Saens, Bruch, and Vivaldi. Every night I would spend hours listening to a Bach Partitia or a Haydn concerto on repeat on my MP3 player, hoping one day to play just like Itzhak Perlman or Hilary Hahn at Carnegie Hall in New York City. I had an affinity towards pieces with a faster pace, which I always credited to my swimming background and my obsession with speed. Mr. Dempsey got so frustrated with me when I rushed; for two weeks straight he made me go through every lesson and practice with a metronome.

Classical music was always my favorite. The elegance with which the notes flowed from the pages and the history of each composer fascinated me. I always used to tell Mr. Dempsey that I would play in Vienna, Austria, one day, which is where Mozart, Beethoven, Schubert, and Brahms spent much of their time composing and studying. It was also the birthplace of my great-grandfather, who had handmade a violin in 1899 that was passed down to me once I grew into it, and is still my instrument of choice today. Mr. Dempsey would always look at me and say, "Si, Vivace, you will. And I will be there, sitting in the crowd with a metronome, making sure you aren't rushing." He laughed every single time he said that and I laughed too, knowing that if I ever played in Vienna he would be there to support me. The violin gave me a sense of calm like nothing else did, and I never felt left out like I did at swim practice. Practicing the violin every day was something that I looked forward to, and when nothing in my swimming future was definite, I still had Mr. Dempsey and music.

After Josh left, there were people from USA Swimming who contacted my parents. I was on their radar due to my early success in the sport, and they knew we were in a tough spot. They strongly suggested that we consider moving somewhere with more training options. Florida, Texas, and California predominantly and consistently produce the best American athletes when it comes to Olympic swimming. They suggested we move to one of those states, explaining how my training options would expand exponentially. After the phone call, my parents were willing to consider that course of action. After a lot of research and many lengthy discussions, my parents were most drawn to Pine Crest. Located in Fort Lauderdale, Florida, Pine Crest was a well-known team where I could train at the level I required. It was also a boarding school, so I could train and go to school in Fort Lauderdale while my mom, dad, and Danny stayed in Rhode Island. It wasn't the ideal setup for any of us, but it was a viable option and my parents planned a visit to Pine Crest so that we could check it out together.

The morning of our trip, our luggage was packed, and Danny had already been sent to stay with my grandparents. Originally, I had told my parents I was willing to consider moving. I wanted to be open to whatever it took to make me the best. But something happened as we were eating breakfast together in our kitchen, just as we had so many times before. I realized the actuality of what moving would mean. I would leave Rhode Island, the place that had always been my home. I would pick up my entire life to live somewhere I had never been, and my family and my best friends would become people I saw only once in a while. As that sunk in, I became convinced of one thing; I wouldn't do it. My gut churned and I reverted to my old days as "The Fuss" and threw the loudest, most forceful tantrum of my life. It didn't matter what my parents said, I wasn't going. My delivery may have been poor, but my reasoning was rational and ultimately my parents agreed. I had become one of the best swimmers in the nation by training in Rhode Island. I wanted the Olympics more than anything, but something told me that I didn't have to leave behind everything and everyone I knew to live out my dreams. The last Olympic swimmer from Rhode Island competed in the 1948 Olympics. I was determined to end that dry spell, and moving to Florida would strip me of that chance. Maybe Florida would be amazing, maybe it wouldn't. But deep down there was no doubt in my mind, Rhode Island was where I belonged. We never boarded our flight to Fort Lauderdale.

Ultimately, after that day, the Bluefish Swim Club in Attleboro, Massachusetts, became my only real option. I had a five day trial period with the team the first week of September, but by day two I knew I had made the right decision. Carl Cederquist would be my coach, and he had an incredible reputation within New England Swimming for producing the best athletes in my age-group. I loved him from the second I met him. He was an exuberant man who reminded me of Santa Claus, but instead of a beard he had a white mustache, sandy colored hair, and rosy cheeks. His enthusiasm was contagious and from my very first practice with Bluefish, he made me feel like a valued member of the team. I recognized most of the other swimmers from prior meets. I had never been able to get to know them since we had swum against one another, but now we were teammates. They welcomed me with open arms, and the best part was that I could swim with kids who were my age and my caliber, unlike at Rams. The transition was a remarkably easy one, and it seemed I had fallen into the best case scenario. I had people my own age to train with, an amazing coach who believed in me once again, and I was able to stay in Rhode Island with my family and friends.

I couldn't have been happier that I was at Bluefish, training under Carl, with my new teammates. But it was definitely a stretch for my parents, although they never made it seem like an inconvenience. I had swim practice six days a week, so my mom or dad would have to drive the 45 minutes to and from the pool, take me to violin and piano lessons every week, and I had ballet on the weekends. My activities also had to be balanced with Danny's sports, which consisted of soccer and track, and that spread our family thin. We had less time to spend together, but my parents always put us first, and never made us feel like keeping up with our packed schedules was a big deal.

That year passed by remarkably fast. I loved practice, I excelled at swimming, I made new friends, and I continued to build my relationship with Carl. Everything that Josh had taught me made it easy to reach the next level, and my times only continued to get faster. Violin also continued to be a large part of my life. I kept taking lessons with Mr. Dempsey on Friday afternoons before swim practice, which was another reason why I was happy to stay in Rhode Island. My progress was slower than it had been during that month of August the previous summer, but I was still working my way through an array of more advanced pieces, and Mr. Dempsey was pleased with my progress. I would play violin for an hour every day before school, come home from school and practice piano for 30 minutes, and then do my homework in the car on the ride to swim practice. There was not a single minute of my day that wasn't put to good use. Even now, I credit my ability to be constantly productive to the countless activities I did growing up. I have incredible time management skills, and that's because for so long, it was the only thing I knew.

As the swimming season finished, I was the only member of my team to qualify for Junior Nationals. The meet was held at Stanford University, where Lea Loveless coached. I was elated. Qualifying for Junior Nationals was the first step in the trajectory to potentially making an Olympic Team, and the meet couldn't have gone better. I won the 200 backstroke at 11 years old. I was the youngest Junior National Champion ever, and I was beyond thrilled with my performance. I did well in my other events, but I was certainly starting to become known for my ability in backstroke. The swimmer who placed second was 18, and I couldn't help but wonder, if I kept training, how much I could improve by the time I turned 18. At 11 that seemed like a million years away, but it was still fun to think about. And considering that I won my first Junior National Title at the same university where the Olympic gold medalist Lea Loveless coached seemed serendipitous. It reminded me of when I had broken her record as a seven-year old and reinforced the magic that could happen with hard work and serious training. I returned to Rhode Island more inspired and motivated than ever before.

The next year I remained committed to my various sports and music lessons. But I continued to take violin and swimming the most seriously. While the other activities gave me a more solid perspective and balance than singularly focusing on one thing would have, the violin and swimming were the areas in which I inarguably possessed the most natural talent. On the violin, I progressed from more basic concertos and sonatas to Bach Partitias. I continued to practice every morning for an hour and tried to fit two hours in on the weekends. I was named Concertmaster of the Ocean State Youth Orchestra, which was open to anyone under the age of 18. We would play at beautiful concert halls throughout Rhode Island, and it gave me a small taste of what it would be like to perform professionally one day. But no matter how much I daydreamed about playing in pristine venues around the world with a renowned orchestra, that vision faded away every time I dove into the pool. I loved the violin, but when it came down to choosing one over the other, swimming always won out.

Swimming was starting to become more intense too. Carl saw my potential for improvement and continued to challenge me. The intervals were faster, the sets were longer, and the practices were at times grueling, even though I loved pushing myself to the max when it came to training. Keeping up in school was starting to become difficult, because I was leaving for swim meets at least once or twice a month for days at a time. I had always prided myself on getting straight A's, but that was proving to be harder to swing with numerous activities pulling me in varying directions.

At 12, I found myself back at Junior Nationals, which was held in Irvine, California. Again, I was the only one from Bluefish who had qualified, but when I arrived, I was pleasantly surprised to see my old friend, Laura Sogar, who had stayed with the Rams Swim Club. We were both on our own, so we spent all of our free time catching up and hanging out. Having a friend to cheer for made the experience even more special, and I had the meet of my life. Carl made training fun and found thoughtful ways to motivate me, just like Josh had, and I was swimming faster than ever. My times were improving astronomically, and I won the 200 IM, the 400 IM, the 200 backstroke, and I placed in the top eight in all of my other events. By the time the meet was finished, I was over the moon with happiness. Not only had I been reunited with my old friend, but I had done my absolute best at that meet.

After losing Josh as a coach, contemplating moving, and working into the routine at Bluefish, the dust had finally settled, and I loved where I had landed. Carl and my teammates at Bluefish were like family, and my swimming career was taking off with more momentum than I could have hoped. After my second Junior National meet, I was flying high. I had worked so hard to get to that point and with Carl as my coach I felt unstoppable. My mind fast-forwarded to what I might be able to achieve in the future with this sort of focus and dedication. I had set my sights on being the best in the world, and now with four Junior National titles under my belt at the age of 12, that goal was slowly becoming more and more realistic. Nothing could ruin the sheer joy that flooded through me after that meet—or so I thought.

At the end of Junior Nationals, after I had high-fived with the other swimmers and hugged Laura goodbye, yet again, my world came crashing down. I don't remember how exactly I found out, but I can still feel the blinding rage that took over when I heard the news. A man named Chuck Batchelor had bought Bluefish Swim Club. At first, I didn't care. The owner of the swim club didn't make any difference to me. But then I found out that starting the next year, Chuck would take over as my coach and Carl would work with other swimmers. I felt totally and completely blindsided, just like when I had heard Josh was leaving. My mom tried to comfort me, but there was nothing she could do. I had heard of Chuck before, and I knew he had an outstanding reputation as a coach and produced phenomenal swimmers. But I didn't care. I had made so much progress working with Carl, and the last thing I wanted was to work with anyone else.

I dug my heels into the floor. I wouldn't swim for Chuck. It wasn't fair to me or Carl. When Josh had been ripped away from me, I was heartbroken. But I wasn't 10 years old anymore. I had never met Chuck, but I'd already made up my mind. I resolved that there was no way I would swim for him. The problem was, as it turned out, I didn't have any say in the matter. He now owned the team, and it was either get coached by Chuck or move to Florida. I loathed the idea of having to swim for yet another new coach, but I had no choice but to suck it up.

The first day of practice as a 13-year-old, I walked onto the pool deck with my jaw clenched and my head down. I had already decided, from the moment I heard he was taking Carl's place as my coach, that I wanted nothing to do with him. He had jet black hair and a full, jet black beard to match. He wore dark rimmed glasses and always sported eccentric colorful Hawaiian shirts and Croc shoes, which I thought looked ridiculous. From day one, I did nothing but acknowledge his presence, and even that was a struggle. To make matters worse, I was back to being the youngest in my group without anyone to train with my own age. I was undeniably bitter about the setup. My group practiced at the same time as Carl's group. I was coached by Chuck with new senior swimmers who he had brought with him in lanes one, two, three, and four. But I watched wistfully as all of my friends swam in lanes five, six, seven, and eight with Carl. I would have given anything to be back in that group with the teammates and coach who had become like family to me. But I was forced into a new reality.

The 45-minute drive to and from practice hadn't felt like a big deal before. But now that I was once again on my own with a bunch of older swimmers and paired with a coach I could hardly even look at, the drive seemed to take forever. To make matters worse, I wasn't the biggest fan of the way Chuck's workouts were laid out. He would write a full practice set on the board at the front of the pool, and we were expected to get in and swim full force with absolutely no warm-up. The entire time I had been swimming, I had never been asked to swim serious intervals without having a proper warm-up. I found it impossible to jump in and reach my threshold speed immediately after not touching the water for a full 24 hours. But just like when Chuck became my coach, I had no input in how the workouts were designed. So I begrudgingly jumped in and swam the sets he designed without the luxury of a warm-up, as I watched Carl coach my friends.

This routine went on for approximately three months, and during that time I don't think I said more than an obligatory hello to

Chuck. He was putting in such a valiant effort to get to know me and make me feel comfortable, but I wouldn't budge. Those months were gloomy for me, and I felt as if swimming had been tainted. Sure, I still wanted to get in the water, but I didn't want to do it for Chuck. After training began, meets quickly followed and after I swam my events, I would maneuver my way through the mesh of swimmers and coaches on deck in search of Carl. I was always eager to hear what Carl had to say about my performance, and I could barely wait to find him once I had completed a race. Only after speaking to Carl would I then find Chuck for a secondary opinion. But one Saturday afternoon at a meet at Harvard University, he confronted me after I had gone up to Carl for the third time that day.

As soon as I saw Chuck standing over me, I frowned. "Elizabeth, you know that I'm your coach," he said. I had expected him to be stern, but he didn't seem angry. If anything, he actually seemed hurt. He had put in such an effort to coach me and make me the best athlete possible, but I had completely disregarded that effort for months.

But I was stubborn, and I still wasn't ready to let down my guard. "I never wanted to change coaches." I placed my hands on my hips. "I want to swim for Carl."

I noticed Chuck's posture change when I said that. He stood up a little straighter, narrowed his eyes, and gave me an ultimatum. "You need to give me a chance, Elizabeth. If you're not willing to do that, then you need to find somewhere else to swim." I could tell by the look on his face that he was serious, and he didn't wait for my answer after he spoke. I stared at the back of his brightly colored shirt as he walked away, unsure of what to do. Ultimately, the reality was that there wasn't another team of that caliber in New England. I had no choice. I was going to have to give Chuck a chance.

CHAPTER FOUR

I spent a lot of time considering what Chuck had said. He was right. It was pointless to swim for a coach who I wouldn't listen to. The problem was I didn't know how to let go of the negative feelings festering inside me. Then I had an idea. The next week, I walked into practice with a mission. I marched out onto the pool deck and went directly to Chuck. If I was going to give him a chance, I had to know he'd be willing to work with me. "I need you to start implementing a warm-up in practice," I said matter-of-factly. "It's not just me that has a problem with it, it's everybody." He looked me in the eye, nodded ever so slightly, and the next practice written on the board before the main set, was a warm-up.

Chuck had met me halfway, and I was over the moon. It was a relief to really start training again. Before I had just been going through the motions at practice and completing the required sets, wishing I was in Carl's group. But once Chuck and I made that deal, I started giving swimming my all again and listening to what he had to say. He wasn't like Carl or Josh. Chuck knew how to push my buttons; he also knew how to push me to my limits and beyond. He was by far the best coach that I had ever swum for, and he transformed me as an athlete. That first year was a difficult one, and it wasn't uncommon for me to get out of the pool in the middle of practice, scream at him, and walk out. But there was no doubt that he made me a better swimmer.

That April we went to a meet in Charlotte, North Carolina, and I made my first Grand Prix Final in the 200 backstroke. I placed third and was elated. I couldn't believe it and as I stared at my name on the scoreboard, I was flying high. However, I didn't realize that my third place finish would result in a mandatory drug test. The second I got out of the pool there was a woman waiting with a clipboard. "You have 60 minutes to report to drug testing," she told me with no further explanation.

I had no idea what that would entail, but I quickly found out that drug testing requires removing all of your clothing and urinating in front of a complete stranger. I felt entirely exposed. In fact, I was so nervous that it took me over an hour to produce a urine sample. When I was finally done, I was still feeling uncomfortable about the entire experience. Because I was the only swimmer my age who had qualified for the meet, I was with four of my 18-year-old teammates who had also qualified. I was relieved to join them along with Chuck who had been waiting on me for dinner. When I jumped into the van, instead of congratulating me on a great race like I expected, the guys were immediately on my case for making them wait.

"Take your time, Beisel. It's not like we're hungry at all."

"Did you have trouble peeing in your diaper? Should we call your mommy?"

"If I swim slow tomorrow it's because of you."

I felt tears welling up behind my eyes. I could barely take a deep breath, because I knew if I did I would immediately start sobbing. What was already a rollercoaster of a night had just become even worse, and I felt the same sense of exclusion I had swimming with the older members of Rams years ago. Was this what it was going to be like every time I swam fast?

A million thoughts were swirling around in my mind when Chuck's loud voice cut in. "Hey, listen up. When you guys are fast enough to get drug tested, then you can give her a hard time. Until that happens, lay off."

I leaned back in my seat, grateful that Chuck had my back. After that night, any resentment I had held towards him disappeared completely. I was swimming better than I ever had before, and he had earned my trust. Chuck was my coach, and I didn't want to swim for anyone else.

That year, at the end of the season instead of going to Junior Nationals, at 13, I made the 2006 USA Swimming Nationals. I was the youngest swimmer to qualify for the meet, and I had no idea what to expect. Junior Nationals had been great preparation, but Nationals was a whole new level. I would be swimming in a meet with some of the best swimmers in the entire world. Natalie Coughlin, Michael Phelps, and Ryan Lochte were my idols. I had grown up watching them swim on television, and they would all be there competing. Nationals was also different because if you placed top two in your event, the meet wasn't over as it was at Junior Nationals. The top two swimmers in each event made the National Team and automatically qualified for the Pan Pacific Championships later that summer.

Before boarding our flight to California, where Nationals would be held, Chuck looked at me. "You can make Pan Pacs this year," he said. I rolled my eyes. I was only 13, and it was my first time ever going to Nationals. To have even qualified for the meet at that age was an anomaly—making the National Team and being able to represent the United States of America at the Pan Pacific Championships seemed like a massive long shot. "I'm serious," he insisted.

I shook my head, grabbed my luggage, and didn't think any more about what he said. I had enough on my mind trying to imagine what Nationals would be like and making a list of all the big name swimmers who I wanted to get autographs from.

When I first arrived at the meet, butterflies danced in my stomach. Everyone else seemed so much older, bigger, and more qualified. I was great compared to the other swimmers at Bluefish Swim Club, but these were the fastest swimmers in the country and many had already won National titles and even Olympic medals. I felt a deep sense of honor to have the opportunity to be there surrounded by so many accomplished athletes, and I quietly observed. Because Nationals was located in Irvine that year and it was summertime, all of the races took place under a sunny California sky. I loved that the meet was able to be held outdoors. Taking in a breath of fresh air, I looked around. I couldn't help but notice the chiseled bodies of the more seasoned swimmers, and I felt small and inexperienced in comparison.

I stuck close to Chuck as I waited for the 200 backstroke. I watched in awe, as the events began, and listened to the booming voices of the commentators over the microphones—race after race. I tried to take in every detail; the blue and white USA Swimming flags, the way the swimmers plowed through the pool from one wall to the other with brilliant technique, and the excitement which buzzed throughout the maze of people. It was overwhelming in a way that made me feel inspired, like a beautiful piece of music or a powerful film. I barely spoke a word because I was so intent on soaking it all in. When it came time to swim in the preliminaries, as usual, I took my place in the water. I had swum the 200 backstroke so many times that I knew every movement. Each stroke was calculated, concise, and came automatically. I didn't have to think about anything, all I had to do was replicate what I had practiced day in and day out. Going in, I wanted to do my best. I hoped my time would be fast enough that I could advance to finals that night. And it was. I qualified first in the preliminaries.

When I had arrived at the pool in Irvine I was calm, cool, and collected. It was my first Nationals and I was happy just to be part of the meet, but I had felt almost like a bystander. After finishing first in prelims, I went from having zero expectations to being a real contender for the National Team. My heart pounded faster and faster as I thought about finals later that night and my palms began to sweat. I was so fidgety I had to sit on my hands; I had never been that anxious in my entire life. How did I even get here? I was a middle-schooler. My friends were probably going to the movies or having their parents drop them off at the mall. I was about to swim for a spot on the USA National Team, and I was up against Margaret Hoelzer, a 23-year-old and the American record holder in that event. The rest of the day leading up to finals, I was a nervous wreck. The time before my race that evening crept by slowly, and minutes felt like hours. I just wanted to get finals over with but at the same time the apprehension of what the outcome would be was crushing. Before I went out for my race, Chuck turned towards me. "Do you remember what I told you about Pan Pacs?"

Thinking back to when I had rolled my eyes at the idea of qualifying for the Pan Pacifics and making the National Team, I nodded. "Yes."

"You're doing it tonight," Chuck said. That was the last thing he told me before I swam. I don't recall anything about that race; I completely blacked out. I went so much harder and faster than usual that I miscounted my strokes into the finish and ended the race by bashing my head on the wall instead of my hand. All I remember is hitting the wall with my head, looking up at the giant scoreboard, and seeing the number two beside my name. Margaret Hoelzer won, but my second place finish had secured me a spot on the USA Swimming National Team at 13 years old. That made me the youngest National Team swimmer on record. After our race, Margaret and I sat down for a joint interview. I had no idea what to do or say, so I just tried to answer whatever the interviewer asked honestly. After a few questions, she turned to Margaret. "What's it like to race someone who's 10 years younger than you?" It felt just like when I had to swim with the older swimmers back at the Rams Swim Club and when Chuck had switched me out of Carl's group and into the senior lanes. Once again, I was the odd duck out—stuck in an awkward position in which I had no real peers. That morning, watching all of the older, bigger, more experienced swimmers, I hadn't felt like I belonged. And that was something that even making the USA National Team didn't necessarily change.

I was proud of my accomplishment and excited to make the National Team. But when I joined the rest of the swimmers for a mandatory two week training camp in Santa Barbara before Pan

Pacific Championships, I felt even younger and smaller than I had at Nationals. There were no other 13 year olds on the team, and I longingly thought back to the days when I swam with Laura and we went on and on about our favorite animals and the latest Harry Potter book in the locker room. But I did love the practices and was assigned to one of the National Team coaches, Gregg Troy. Coach Troy was a short man with salt and pepper hair, a bald spot, and a mustache. He was one of the greatest coaches in the world and was known for being Ryan Lochte's coach at the University of Florida. I even got to swim in the same lane as Ryan, whose poster hung on my bedroom wall. I was so intimidated by Ryan that I could barely muster up the courage to ask him what the intervals were during a set. In my eyes he was a superstar, and I was swimming in the same lane with him on the USA National Team. It was literally a dream come true. Work-outs were never the problem, it was everything else. Without anyone on the team even close to my age, I spent almost all of my free time on my own. The more senior swimmers seemed to have an admirable rapport with one another, and they broke off into groups and socialized outside of practice. But there wasn't anyone for me to talk to, and I didn't know how to connect with my teammates. I put my head down outside of the pool and kept to myself. When I wasn't swimming, I felt invisible.

All of my meals I ate alone or sat silently at the end of the table. I thought the absolute world of the other swimmers; they were my heroes. I just had no idea what to talk to them about. I couldn't ask them for their autographs like I had planned, because I quickly learned that was a huge faux pas within the National Team. At least that's what I overheard from two girls talking about it in the bathroom. So, I simply said nothing. One day I was sitting at a table alone, as usual. I had developed a strategy and tried to eat every meal as fast as humanly possible so I could go back to my room. Sitting by myself was never fun, and I hated that I had no friends. But as I was about to get up, Natalie Coughlin came over and sat down across from me. "Hi there!" She said with a huge smile.

For a moment, I froze. Legendary Olympic swimmer, Natalie Coughlin, was sitting two feet away from me. I had watched her win gold in the 100 backstroke at the 2004 Olympic Games in Athens and idolized her. Now she was talking to me. I almost turned around just to be sure she wasn't saying hello to someone else.

"I don't think we've officially met yet. I'm Natalie," she continued.

"Hi…I'm Elizabeth," I stuttered.

"It's so nice to meet you. Welcome to camp. I'm sorry we haven't had a chance to chat. How are you doing? What do you think about training?" She asked.

Natalie sat there with me for almost an hour. She wanted to know how practices were going, what I liked to do outside of swimming, and what I thought about Santa Barbara. She was warm and funny, and the fact that she went out of her way to make me feel comfortable changed everything. That conversation with Natalie Coughlin was the highlight of my trip. At 13, I recognized what she had exemplified when she didn't have to—leadership. When I had no one to talk to and felt raw and vulnerable as the youngest member of the team, she reached out and made me feel like I belonged. After that talk with Natalie, I didn't become instant best friends with everyone on the team, but I no longer felt completely alone. After she left, I promised myself that if I was ever in the position to make that difference for someone else, I would do it. Natalie may have been an Olympic gold medalist, but she was also down-to-earth, kind, and approachable. If I ever made it as far as she had in swimming, I wanted to be the same way. After that day, I walked around with a little bit more confidence and pride even outside of the pool. Maybe I was the youngest and the smallest, but I was still part of Team USA.

One of the amazing perks of being a Team USA athlete is all the free gear you receive. On the second to last day of camp in Santa Barbara, we were called down to a massive ballroom in the hotel to go through a procedure called "processing." I wasn't particularly excited about this "processing" thing because it inconveniently took place in the middle of my nap time. I reluctantly made my way downstairs to the ballroom, hoping whatever it was wouldn't take too long. Once I opened the double doors, my eyes nearly bulged out of their sockets. It looked like Christmas. USA gear was stacked on top of dozens of tables—swimsuits, caps, goggles, sweatshirts, sneakers, pants, jackets, and backpacks. Anything and everything I could have ever wanted as a swimmer was lined up in front of me. A woman was there to greet me at the door and told me to grab a shopping cart and take one of everything. I couldn't believe how lucky I was. Every article of clothing prominently displayed the American Flag, which solidified how fortunate I was to be representing the United States of America. I quickly made my way through the arrangement of tables, grabbing one (or sneakily, maybe two in some instances) of everything, oohing and awing as I went.

The swim caps were the last item waiting for me at the end of my shopping spree, and they were by far my favorite piece of gear. The black and white swim caps weren't all that exciting on their own, but these donned the American flag along with my last name clearly printed on each side. Seeing that cap with my country's flag and my name on it, I knew that I was officially a member of the USA National Team. I was ecstatic. So much so that the second I got back to my room, I put the cap on my head and walked around in it for at least half an hour, staring incredulously at myself in the mirror. I couldn't wait to get to Pan Pacs and race.

The Pan Pacific Championships is an international meet, and in 2006 it was held in Victoria, British Columbia, Canada. It happens once every four years and serves as Team USA's qualifier for the World Championships the following year. At the end of Pan Pacs, USA Swimming takes the two fastest times of each event from Nationals and Pan Pacs in order to decide the World Championship team for the next year. Going into Pan Pacs, I was the second fastest 200 backstroker in the United States. But Pan Pacs was different than any other international meet. All qualifiers have the option to sign up to compete in any event they want, giving competitors the unique ability to knock other swimmers out of their "qualified" events. For me, this meant swimming the 100 and 200 backstroke, and the 200 and 400 IM. Swimming the extra events was a fun challenge, but my main focus was on maintaining my second place spot for the 200 backstroke in order to qualify for the World Championship team the next year.

When we arrived at the Pan Pacs in Victoria, my jaw dropped instantly. It was by far the biggest arena I had ever seen, and I was amazed by the facility's grandeur. We did a lap around the pool, listening to the managers point out where drug testing, the mixed zone (where the media and athletes mix to conduct interviews), the ready room (where swimmers sit before they are called out before their race), and the warm-down pools were located. I couldn't believe my eyes. Iconic swimmers from other countries like Australia, China, Canada, and Japan swam up and down in the competition pool. I recognized some of the names on their caps from watching them on television at the 2004 Olympic Games in Athens. As once again the youngest, and as an internationally inexperienced swimmer, looking around, it was hard to convince myself that I was capable of competing at that level. But I tried not to let my apprehensions drag me down.

Race day arrived faster than I had anticipated. The 200 backstroke was the first day, which in comparison to other swim meets was atypical. But if anything, I was happy about the schedule modification. I was so excited to finally race and wear my official USA "Beisel" cap. I preferred the black caps, so I put one in my bag and then added in three spare black "Beisel" caps just in case one ripped or got lost before my race. I got to the pool the usual two hours before my race time and warm-up was nothing short of chaotic. The Chinese swimmers had absolutely no order when it came to circle swimming in the lanes, and between the Americans swimming counter-clockwise, and the Australians swimming clockwise, it seemed impossible to have a successful warm up.

The night before Chuck had called and assured me that not only was I ready to race but that I could make the World Championship Team. Before that day, while I had been nervous, I had kept my emotions in check. But with the stress of warm-ups and the pressure of race day, my nerves were beginning to take over. I kept telling myself all I had to do was put up a top eight time in the morning to move on to finals, but the actuality of competing against the best swimmers in the world was daunting. I wished Chuck were there to give me last minute advice and to boost my confidence. I was awesome at Bluefish and I was good at Nationals, but top eight at Pan Pacs and qualifying for the World Championships seemed overwhelmingly unattainable.

I walked to the locker room to change into my racing suit, hoping my anxiety would go away. I pulled and tugged on my skin tight Nike racing suit until it was finally on properly, then returned to our warm-up area to grab my things and get ready to race. When I opened my backpack the first thing I saw was my USA "Beisel" cap. Suddenly all of my doubt melted away. Seeing my name on that cap right next to the American flag was the affirmation I needed. It was literally there, written in black and white, and excitement replaced the trepidation that had plagued me all morning. I was ready to swim. I pulled the black cap over my untamed curly hair and made my way to the ready room.

The ready room was where swimmers went to wait to be called for their race. You were herded into a small space with the people you would be racing against, and it was unnerving to say the least. I had heard horror stories about the ready room and what went on. Some people would try to intimidate you by air boxing, others would sit quietly and stare at you, and some would be standing in the corner throwing up in a trash can because they were so nervous. As I walked in, I saw the seven other competitors in my heat. One of them was Natalie Coughlin. She gave me a huge wave and smile, motioning for me to come and sit next to her. She was in the middle of asking me how my warm-up went, when she looked at my capped head and stopped mid-thought.

"Wait, Beisel, you can't be wearing that cap."

I looked at her confused. Did I accidentally grab someone else's cap and put it on?

"Geez, did no one tell you?" Natalie continued.

"Tell me what?" I asked.

"It's always white caps in the morning for preliminaries and black caps at night for finals. It's been a tradition for decades. I can't believe no one said anything. You have to find a white cap, now!"

I was floored. I couldn't believe the color of my cap mattered so much. And if it was such a big deal, why didn't anyone tell me about it? A moment ago, that cap had given me the assurance I needed. Now I was more nervous than ever. I was going to have to check out of the ready room and grab a white cap from one of my teammates in the team area, which was a three minute walk away. I kept thinking to myself, Why didn't I bring the white ones? What was I thinking? I glanced at the clock; I had six minutes until I was up to swim. There was no way I could miss my first race representing the United States. I sprinted to the team area and frantically searched through people's backpacks, hoping someone would have a white cap. Nothing. Finally, in a random bag I found a white cap covered in flowers. With no time to spare I grabbed the cap, turned it inside out, and ran at full speed back to the ready room. I made it with only 30 seconds to spare. Natalie helped me put it on, and still catching my breath, I paraded out to the pool for my first race as a USA National Team member.

I set up my start, and exploded off the wall once I heard the buzzer. As soon as I was back in my element and swimming, the anxiety disappeared. My strokes were smooth and my mind calmed. My execution was clean, my stroke count was right on target, and when I made my last turn, I knew I was at the very front of the pack. When I touched the wall, I saw the number two next to my name. I was relieved. Not only did I qualify top eight for finals, but I beat my own best time in the process.

That evening, when I warmed up for my race I felt strong and powerful in the water. After overcoming all the stress of the morning and still hitting a personal record I had a good feeling going into finals. I knew if I did my best, I had a real chance to qualify for the World Championships the next year. Not to mention, I couldn't wait to finally race in my USA "Beisel" cap against the fastest 200 backstrokers in the world.

I had thought the prelims ready room was intense that morning, but that was nothing compared to finals. In prelims people talk and laugh in the ready room, saying hello and catching up. It was still intimidating, but fairly low-key. At finals it was a different story. Everyone was silent, wearing big bulky headphones or looking straight down at the ground. I could feel the nervous energy the moment I walked in. I sat down next to Margaret Hoelzer and started talking to her. Margaret was the American record holder in the 200 backstroke who I had swum against in Nationals, and someone I wildly looked up to. She was instantly encouraging and told me to go out there, have fun, and to swim my own race. Talking to Margaret made me forget about the rest of the room, and a few minutes later the announcer told us it was time to walk out. Margaret looked at me. "Let's go to World Champs together next year."

I clung to that sentence the entire race. All I wanted to do was qualify for the World Championships, and this was my one shot. The swim went by remarkably fast, and when I touched the wall I glanced up at the scoreboard and saw the number five next to my name. Fifth? That's it? My heart sank, but I looked at the board again. All I had to do was be the second fastest American, and even with a fifth place finish I had done that. Wow. I had gone a best time by over a second, qualifying me for my first World Championships. Margaret had won the race, and came over to my lane to congratulate me. "See you at Worlds, Beisel. I knew you could do it."

CHAPTER FIVE

I was the youngest swimmer ever to make the USA Swimming National Team and I had successfully qualified for World Championships, but I still had to start high school. I was just as anxious and excited as every other freshman when I walked into my first day at North Kingstown High School. I was becoming known within the world of swimming, but back at school I was just like all the other students my age. Most of the first week was filled with icebreakers and introductions and all of the teachers wanted to hear about what everyone had done over the summer. When it was my time to share, I said that I had spent a lot of time swimming in the ocean and got to take a trip to Canada. I omitted the Pan Pacific Championships for the obvious reason that no one had any idea what it was. I figured I could mention it and then try and explain, but I wanted to be normal and fit in just like everyone else. And for the most part I did.

I still trained six days a week at Bluefish Swim Club with Chuck but going into freshman year I had seriously cut back on my other extracurricular activities. While I loved the diversity of doing lots of different things, I decided to hone in on what I enjoyed most and what I was best at; that left swimming, piano, and violin. So, while swimming and school intensified, I was able to narrow my focus so that I could excel in those areas. World Championships wasn't until March, which meant I had lots of time to train before my next high profile event. I was just settling into my routine at my new school that September when Chuck pulled me aside.

"Elizabeth, Laura Sogar is going to be swimming with the team for a week or so. She's interested in possibly joining Bluefish. I want you to show her the ropes and make sure she feels comfortable. Do you think you can do that?"

I could barely keep from screaming with joy. "Yes, of course!" I was beyond excited to catch up with Laura and was hopeful at the prospect of having someone close to my own age to swim with. Laura was only a year older, and she was also quickly becoming one of the best swimmers in the country. I knew that not only could she could keep up with my times but that she would push me in practice. Not to mention, I had missed her since I had left the Rams. Of course, we saw each other occasionally at meets, but getting to see her every day at practice again would be amazing. When she arrived at Bluefish Swim Club the first day, it was as if we were able to immediately pick up where we had left off. Laura was instantly sold on Bluefish and I was grateful to have her as a teammate. Once she officially joined the team, I felt a sense of belonging that I hadn't experienced since I had swum for Carl with swimmers my own age. Laura and I quickly became inseparable and her being part of the team only made me look forward to going to practice that much more.

The time flew by, and before I knew it, I was trying to explain to my teachers what World Championships was and why I was going to have to miss three full weeks of school. "It's the World Championships for swimming," I said over and over.

But no one really got it. "Oh, like for kids? Or for your age group, right?"

I didn't try to elaborate, I liked that my swimming life was compartmentalized in Attleboro where I trained for Chuck and that school was a separate entity. No one at North Kingstown High School really understood my swimming accolades, and that was just fine with me. After spending so much time trying to blend in with the older swimmers, I loved being just another kid in the classroom with all of my peers. When I left for World Championships, I felt a solid sense of balance in my swimming and personal life. I was doing well at school, I had Laura to swim with at Bluefish, and I was eager to attend my first World Championships.

That year World Championships was held in Melbourne, Australia. The meet was eight days long and before competing we had to attend a mandatory two week training camp so we could acclimate to the time change and bond as a team. We were told in advance that this would be a particularly large scale event because in Australia, swimming is one of the premiere sports, second only to maybe rugby. The event was going to be held in the Rod Laver Arena which is usually where the Australian Open tennis tournament takes place. However, for the 2007 World Championships the tennis court, which sat prominently in the center of stands that seated literally thousands of people, was temporarily turned into a pool. There were over 2,000 swimmers from 167 different nations, and every single session was sold out. If I thought Pan Pacs was huge, World Championships was enormous.

However, I was back to my isolated disposition of not having anyone who I really felt connected to on the World Championship Team. At 14 years old and 115 pounds, I looked and felt completely out of place. When we first arrived in Melbourne, the girl I was assigned to room with requested to stay with someone else. Already, I felt left out and uncertain of my role as a member of the World Championship Team. The next youngest person on the team was Katie Hoff, the iconic American swimmer, and she was 18. In training I swam in the same lane as Katie. At the time, Katie was by far the most dominant female swimmer in the world, and I looked up to her tremendously. She quickly became the closest friend I had on the team. Even though she was four years older, we got along well and she always went out of her way to be friendly and encourage me. I loved the swimming, but again—it was everything else that I found intimidating. We had three nights leading up to the meet where we could get dinner on our own and walk around the city. Everyone else was excited for some free time, but I wasn't looking forward to being all alone in a foreign country far from home. One the first of those free nights I was sitting in my hotel room by myself planning on getting room service. As I was about to pick up the phone to call down and place my order, I heard a knock on the door. I jumped up from my bed and opened it, only to see Katie standing in the entryway. I was speechless.

"Hey, do you have dinner plans?" Katie asked.

"No…I don't." I said embarrassed.

"Perfect!" Katie exclaimed. "Would you like to come to dinner with me and a couple other girls? We'd love if you joined."

"Really?" I asked.

"Of course," she said. "It will be fun."

"Okay…um, yes!" I stammered.

"Great. Get dressed, and I'll wait for you at the elevators."

I closed the door and got ready as fast as I could. I had gone from feeling down in the dumps, pathetically lonely to being over the moon happy. As I pulled on my clothes, my mind was racing. I couldn't believe that Katie Hoff had just asked me to dinner. She invited me. Being able to compete in Australia was an incredible opportunity, but for me it had been a lonely trip and other than at practice, this was the first time I felt included as a member of the team. I was so relieved to have people to eat with that I jumped up and down in my room before I went to go meet them.

Having Katie as a support at Worlds in Australia made me more comfortable because I knew she was looking out for me. But I wasn't able to spend as much time with her as I wanted once the meet began because she was swimming so many different events. When it came time to compete, the venue was larger, louder, and more intense than anything I had ever experienced. The meet was structured so that preliminaries were held in the morning, followed by semi-finals in the evening. After semi-finals, the swimmers who qualified swam in the finals the following evening. To qualify for finals, you had to be in the top eight for that event, and as a swimmer for Team USA it's an unspoken assumption that you will make finals.

The stands were packed and every single seat for each session had been completely sold-out. Even in preliminaries the stands were alive with thunderous applause and thousands of people screaming loudly. It seemed like Katie was always in the process of warming up or cooling down, and I spent most of my time on the pool deck alone. Staring at my competitors, I saw Olympians and World Champions who were full-grown adults. I looked down at my stick, thin frame and wondered what I was even doing there. Representing the United States of America suddenly seemed way too significant to take on as a 14-year-old. There was no question in my mind that I was way out of my league. Staring at the screaming fans and the mirage of colors from the various flags which hung proudly over the pool, I just wanted to go home. I missed my family, and I was supposed to be at high school, struggling with chemistry or gossiping with my friends, not about to swim for the USA World Championship Team against people way older, way bigger, and way more experienced.

Representing my country. Those words had been drilled into my head and the magnitude of that responsibility hit me like a freight train the day of my event. I didn't know what to do or how to handle the pressure. And before I went to the ready room, I made my way to the bathroom alone and started vomiting. The nerves were too much, and I was mentally and physically more overwhelmed than I had ever been in my entire life. Once I flushed my breakfast down the toilet, I signed into the ready room and sat with the rest of the swimmers in my heat for the preliminaries. The only event I had qualified for was the 200 backstroke, which was usually a breeze for me. But that day, somehow even my favorite race seemed intimidating as I eyed my competition. There wasn't anything I could do at that point but swim my best, and even though I didn't feel great in the water, I made it to the semifinals that evening.

Making the semifinals should have made me feel better, but it only made me that much more nervous. There wasn't anyone who I could really talk to, so the doubts in my head echoed louder and louder as the day went on. After eating lunch, I threw up everything I ate again. I couldn't keep down any food, and the adrenaline rush as I thought about the race that night kept me wide awake during the time I was usually able to take a nap. My body was shaky, and mentally I wasn't able to focus. When I sat down in the ready room, I felt anything but prepared. Throughout my entire career, I had always been able to rise to the occasion. The size of the meet and my inexperience never seemed to trump my ability to show up when it mattered. But that day, I couldn't get it together.

I had a horrible race and I placed twelfth. There's not a word to describe how low I felt when I realized that I hadn't even made finals. After all of the training and how much work I had put in, making the national team, qualifying for the World Championships and flying across the world to compete, I hadn't even made finals in my only event. Not only had I let down myself, I had let down my teammates, my parents who had given up so much to always get me to practice, the coaches who had worked so hard to make me my best, and worst of all, I had let down my country. I wasn't just swimming as Elizabeth Beisel, I was swimming as a member of the USA World Championship Team, and I hadn't even made it to finals. I was so ashamed and embarrassed. How could I have let that happen?

Everyone on the team was kind and supportive, but I still felt like a complete loser. Not only did I not have any friends, I couldn't even do what I had come to do—swim. Leaving the World Championships in Melbourne, I felt absolutely awful for messing up so badly. When it came to swimming, this was the first time I had ever seriously failed. And I hated the way that felt. I went through that race over and over again in my mind, trying to figure out what I could have done differently and where I went wrong. Then I came to a conclusion. I couldn't go back. I had lost in front of the entire world. And no amount of wishing or worrying was going to change that. But I made a decision after the World Championships—I would never fail to make finals again. My next big event was 15 months away. That was when I would be swimming in my first Olympic Trials, and I made myself a promise right then and there—I would work harder than I had ever worked before. I would make the Olympic team, and the next chance I had to represent the USA I would do better.

CHAPTER SIX

Those 15 months, I kept true to the promise I had made to myself after the World Championships in Melbourne. Once I returned from Australia, I trained harder than I had ever trained before. Violin and piano became less important hobbies, while swimming took center stage in my life. I was still doing well at school and loved spending time with kids my own age. I even had a boyfriend who would meet me at my locker in between classes. But when I got to the pool it was all business. Laura and I pushed one another as trials grew closer and closer. Her best event was breaststroke, and I was definitely a backstroker. So there was a strong sense of comradery between us, and we were never in direct competition with one another. I put everything I had into each and every training session and being able to swim with Laura made practice at Bluefish that much better. Fifteen months seemed to fly by in no time, and before long we were heading to the 2008 Olympic Trials in Omaha, Nebraska.

Six swimmers from Bluefish had qualified for trials, including Laura Sogar and myself. We arrived five days before the first day of competition so that we could get into our hotel rooms, feel out the competition pool, and gain our bearings. After all of the meets where I had spent the majority of my time alone, I was incredibly thankful that I got to room with Laura, who had become one of my very best friends. Olympic Trials is without question the most stressful meet in USA Swimming. Trials is where people's lifelong dreams come true, it's also where they die. Tenths of a second, one bad turn, a hesitation off of the block; years of work can either be made or broken in a mere matter of minutes. The meet was held at the Qwest Center, and from my first warm-up lap in the 10-lane 50-meter pool I couldn't have felt cleaner or stronger in the water. I had been swimming awesome times in practice, and I had a good feeling going into the competition. But I didn't know if I could trust that; after all it was the Olympic Trials. So I tried not to get my hopes up and swam whatever Chuck told me to in practice.

My main events were the 400 IM and the 200 backstroke. The 400 IM was my warm-up event, which would take place on day one. The 200 backstroke was the race that was going to potentially take me to the Beijing 2008 Summer Olympic Games, and that wasn't until four days later. The sequence of my events was ideal, and I knew that I had prepared for trials to the absolute best of my ability. All I had to do was swim my fastest, and I could realistically make it to the Olympic Games in the 200 backstroke at fifteen years old. It was surreal to think about, but deep down I knew that I was ready. However, trials went nothing like I expected.

The day before the beginning of the Olympic Trials, a tornado ripped a section of the roof off of the Qwest Center. In swimming it's protocol that you at least touch the water the day before an event. But instead of getting in a few last laps, resting, and having time to mentally prepare, we spent seven hours in a moldy dark basement seeking shelter with hundreds of other cramped swimmers. It was the biggest meet of my life, I had been swimming my best times, and now here I was spending the day before my first event stuck in some dungeon. Then I thought back to World Championships. I had let my nerves take over, and that had been disastrous. Despite how inconvenient the circumstances were, I knew that I couldn't let anything affect my performance.

No one was happy about the situation, but at least we were all in it together. "You know what?" Chuck said. "I'm glad this happened. You guys needed some rest. I didn't want you swimming today anyhow." We all knew that wasn't the case, but the fact that Chuck remained so positive and calm made us all feel better. If Chuck wasn't worried, then I knew things would work out. And by the next day, the Qwest Center was back in business and we were at the pool for the first day of trials.

Despite the slight setback of the tornado, the Qwest Center was booming with life from the second we entered the arena. The stands were packed and the crowd cheered enthusiastically as some of the most well-known American swimmers and coaches populated the pool deck. The sense of anticipation and the nervous excitement was palpable from my first warm-up. I wanted to make the Olympic team more than absolutely anything, and so did every single swimmer there. The atmosphere was electric; music boomed throughout the arena, fluorescent lighting was used to dramatize the entrance of the swimmers, and the pool was lined with slender pieces of metal which sent orange flames flying to the ceiling when a record was broken.

During World Championships I had psyched myself out, and I wasn't going to let that happen again. Besides, with a good friend by my side and all of the extra training I had put in during the last 15 months, I felt confident and ready. Instead of allowing the ostentatiousness of the event to intimidate me, I fed off of it. I had the chance to prove myself after coming up short of making my event final in World Championships. I had waited 15 months for the opportunity to redeem myself. I let the roar of the crowd energize me and imagined myself shooting off of the block like a firework exploding into the night. Besides, the 400 IM was a no-pressure race for me. Sure, I wanted to qualify for finals that night. But no one expected me to, and it was off of the table for me to qualify for the Olympic Team in that race. All I had to do was jump in and swim, then I could get ready for the 200 backstroke four days later.

This time, waiting in the ready room for the preliminaries, I was able to stay focused. The 400 IM would be over before I knew it, and then maybe if I was lucky, I'd get to swim finals that night. If not, I had plenty of time to prepare for the 200 backstroke. There was nothing to worry about at that point. So, I enjoyed the applause as I entered the blackened stadium and heard my name announced. I shook out my arms, awaited my que, and climbed up on the block. Once I was in the water, everything was easy. The 15 months of training had certainly paid off. My strokes were smoother and more efficient than they had ever been. And as soon as I began that race, I could feel the intensity of my usual rhythm increase as my adrenaline started to take over. When I touched the wall, I felt amazing. I knew I had given it my absolute all, and I glanced up at the scoreboard hoping that I had beat my own best time. The crowd erupted from the stands, although it took me a minute to realize why. I had just beaten the US Olympics Trials Record and swam the fastest time out of anyone in the world for the 400 IM that year.

For a moment, nothing registered, and then I began to feel sick to my stomach. The whole stadium was on their feet cheering for me. But that wasn't supposed to happen. I wasn't even sure if I would make finals, and just like that I went to being the top seed in the 400 IM going into finals that night. That sort of expectation and pressure was something I was prepared to deal with when it came to backstroke, but not now. Not the first day. Not the IM. Although the race was over, my heart kept anxiously thudding in my chest, and as I made my way out of the pool area I could feel my hands start to shake. I had never gone anywhere close to that time in the IM, now everyone would expect me to do it again that night. What if I couldn't? What if I lost and this messed up my mental game and jeopardized my chance at making it in backstroke? What if it was a repeat of the World Championships, and I let everyone down all over again?

My mind was reeling and as much as I tried, I found it impossible to reign in my thoughts. That morning all I had wanted was to make the finals, now I wasn't so sure. I couldn't concentrate on anything for the rest of the day. Everything felt off. I could barely eat, and I couldn't sleep at all when it came to my usual nap. I grabbed some fruit before going to our team meeting before finals, hoping to get something in my system before the race. We sat down, as was routine, and Chuck went over the timeline of the races and let us know what to expect. Then everyone exited the room in a single file line. I still had an apple in my hand when I made it to the door at the very end of the group.

Chuck looked at me. "When you walk back into this room tonight, you'll be an Olympian."

I stared at him skeptically and bit into my apple. Part of me wanted to roll my eyes, part of me wanted to believe him, and all of me thought that making the Olympic team would be a dream come true.

It took everything out of me to composedly make my way to the warm-up area. The Olympic Trials has extraordinarily tight security, with obvious good reason. Only registered coaches, swimmers, and officials are permitted on the pool deck at any time. So when I felt a tap on my shoulder before diving in for warm-up, I expected to see one of my teammates or Chuck. Instead I was standing face-to-face with my boyfriend from North Kingstown High School. "Hey!" he said, grinning. "Are you Elizabeth Beisel?"

I was completely caught off guard. He had probably asked me 10 times if he could come, and every single time I had given him an emphatic no. The sheer pressure of a meet like that alone was enough. Now my boyfriend, who never should have been able to get passed armed security, was standing two feet away from me on deck before the biggest race of my life. "What are you doing here?"

Luckily Chuck immediately took note of what was happening and had him removed, but my concentration had already been thrown. I jumped in and tried to warm-up but my entire body felt tight. My strokes were off, and I couldn't help but replay the last 48 hours in my mind. The tornado, the hours spent hunkering down and not even being able to touch the water the previous day, my unexpected win at preliminaries that morning, and now my high school boyfriend surprising me at the worst possible time. Now I was about to swim in the finals for a spot to compete at the Olympics. The.Olympic.

Games. I had forgotten about trying to control my nerves and let them run rampant.

After my first warm-up I went back to the stands and sat next to Laura. "Hey, Beisel," she said cheerfully. I was in a complete daze, and the only thing I was capable of was staring languidly at the competition pool in front of us. I tried to shut out everything, because the only thoughts I had were telling me that I was in way over my head.

"How are you doing?" She asked after a few minutes.

I didn't even move my gaze from the pool. "I'm so nervous. I think I'm going to throw up."

"No, you won't," she said reassuringly. "You're amazing. You're totally fine, and I know that you've got this. You're going to do great."

I looked at Laura, glanced down at the floor, lifted my head and involuntarily threw up all over her.

Thankfully, Laura is the kindest, most understanding friend anyone could ever ask for. She gave me a bit of an annoyed glance, wiped the throw up off of her jacket, and got back to trying to encourage me. "Alright. Um, well, let's go to the locker room and put on your racing suit."

Unlike World Championships when I had to endure my nervous stomach alone, at least I had Laura. She went with me to the locker room, helped me get on my suit, and made me feel immensely better at one of the most pivotal moments of my swimming career. When I went back out on the pool deck for my last warm-up, I was far from calm, but at least I wasn't throwing up on anyone. It was 30 minutes before my race, and I dove in for my first warm-up before I had to compete in finals and try to replicate my rogue performance from that morning. I had barely swum for a minute when Chuck pulled me out. I got out of the pool and went over to him when he motioned for me.

"What's wrong with you?"

It was easy for him to tell my stroke was off, and I had no

explanation. Chuck and I had gotten so close he could read my emotions through the way I looked when I swam. I didn't know what to say, and the turbulent emotions of the day boiled to the forefront. I started bawling right there on the pool deck. "I can't do this tonight. I just can't. I wasn't ready. I'm sorry. I can't do this."

"Alright," Chuck said seriously. "Why don't we find the girl who got ninth place from this morning and give her your lane tonight? I'm sure she'd love to race."

I'm not sure what I expected Chuck to say, but it certainly wasn't that. I stood there dumbfounded.

"Alright," Chuck crossed his arms over his chest. "You know what? I have someone who's going to make you feel better. Come with me."

Still soaking wet in my racing suit, Chuck led me to a large burly man who was well over six feet tall with bright red curly hair pulled back in a ponytail. "Sit down," Chuck instructed me before he left. "This is Nelson."

As I watched Chuck walk away, I hesitantly sat down next to the man he had pointed out. I didn't know it at the time, but it was Nelson Diebel, the 1992 Olympic gold medalist in the 100 breaststroke. Nelson looked me over, and then he pulled his Olympic gold medal out of his pocket, dangled it in front of my face and said one sentence. "If you do not believe in yourself tonight, then you will never win one of these." With that, he walked away.

I sat on the bench for a moment longer. Despite the chaos of the day and the unexpected turns that trials had handed me, what Nelson said clicked. Sitting there at trials, I realized he was right. If I didn't believe in myself I wasn't going to make it to the Olympics in the IM or backstroke, not now or four years from now. To be an Olympian you have to be the best, and to be the best, you have to be able to show up when it matters the most. What was I doing? That morning I had swum the 400 IM faster than anyone else. I had earned my spot at trials and I was literally minutes away from a race that whether I won or lost, I would remember for the rest of my life.

Nelson's words transformed me. I had three more minutes of warm-up but my attitude changed completely. When I jumped back in the pool, I didn't swim warm-ups as someone who questioned whether or not they should be at that meet, or as a little girl who was smaller and younger than the majority of my competitors. I swam that warm-up as if I was what I wanted to be—an Olympian. I made every stroke intentional and each arm placement was flawless. I thought back to when Josh had taught me the technically perfect version of each stroke, remembered all of the records I had broken, and how I had qualified for Nationals. I was there because I was supposed to be. I went into finals that night with a confidence that I had never possessed before. When they announced my name, I felt certain that I would make the USA Olympic Team. The lights flashed, the music roared, and I climbed onto that starting block like I owned it.

"Take your mark...BEEP."

The buzzer went off, and I threw myself into the water. The 400 IM is known as one of the most grueling but also most interesting races in swimming. It consists of 100 meters of every stroke, following the order of butterfly, backstroke, breaststroke, freestyle. The race leader is constantly changing as swimmers progress through the different strokes, making it one of the most intense to watch. My freestyle and backstroke were by far my strongest strokes, so my only goal was to stay as close to the field as possible when it came to butterfly and breaststroke.

As I was swimming the first 100 meters of butterfly, I felt insanely smooth. Butterfly never came easily for me, but that night I found a rhythm that rocketed me forward. I touched the wall at the front of the pack after fly and quickly made my way through the turn to transition to backstroke. Make your move. Now is your chance. I hadn't expected to be in the lead after the 100 fly, and I knew I had to make the most of my position. I rotated each stroke and dug deep with my hands to push the water down the side of my leg and propel myself forward. The 400 IM is considered a distance event which meant much of my race strategy consisted of "holding back" on the backstroke, so I could save my energy for my weak breaststroke where I knew I would have to sprint just to keep up. But that night there was no holding back.

I harnessed a momentum I had never achieved before, and I had a relentless kick that didn't tire. I kept picturing the end of the race, smiling and knowing my biggest dream had come true. Snap out of it and focus! I told myself as I turned for my second length of backstroke. I peeked underwater to see where I was compared to the rest of the field, and that's when I knew I was the leader—by a lot. I was over a body length ahead of Katie Hoff and only gaining speed. I felt a surge of adrenaline take over. Sorry Chuck, but I'm not listening to your race strategy tonight. I spun my arms as fast as I could and made my way to the other end of the pool to transition to breaststroke, touching a few seconds ahead of Katie. On my underwater pullout, I looked again just to make sure I was still ahead. From the split second glance, I saw that I was in first, Katie was in second, and another girl was not too far behind in third.

I knew breaststroke would be a huge struggle for me, and I did my best to coach myself through those 100 meters. Just stay as close as you can to Katie. She will pass you, but don't freak out. Focus on your tempo. After the first 50 of breaststroke, we turned. I peeked again underwater, only to see that Katie and I were dead even. I couldn't believe it. Stay right with her! Katie started to pull away but not by much, and I couldn't believe the speed I was able to maintain. By the time we got to the wall to turn into our last 100 meters of freestyle, Katie had made up the body length lead I had on her and then some, but I was still at her feet. You still haven't made the team. Don't celebrate yet. The girl in third had crept up on me during the breaststroke leg, and she was gaining on me. The last 100 meters of freestyle was going to be the deciding factor.

Keep going. You can do this. You are so close. I was flailing my arms and legs at that point, swimming the hardest and fastest I had ever swum in my life. At the last turn I checked to see where I was in the lineup. You're still in second. You can be an Olympian in 30 seconds if you just put your head down and race. I thought of all the times Chuck had pushed me in practice, when my body burned so badly that I had wanted to stop, but I kept going. Those practices were to prepare me for this. I wouldn't let my hard work go to waste. I wouldn't fail like I did at World Championships. I felt another burst of energy, and I could see that I was actually making up some ground on Katie. With about 15 meters left, I knew I was going to get second and I was euphoric. I swear, in those last 10 strokes I couldn't help but smile underwater knowing that I had done it. I had put in the hard work and when the stakes were high I had listened to Nelson and believed in myself.

When I hit the wall, I saw the number two next to my name. Just thinking about that race still gives me chills. Of all the races, titles, and even Olympic medals that I've won, that night remains my biggest, best dream come true moment. I had done what I had set out to do. At 15 years old, I was an Olympian. The flames beside the pool shot straight to the ceiling, and the crowd screamed. Katie immediately grabbed me and gave me a huge hug, as we both tried to catch our breath. In the pool, while the crowd was still wildly applauding, she turned to me. "Welcome to the club." I knew exactly what she meant.

CHAPTER SEVEN

No one can prepare you for the Olympics. It doesn't matter how much you train, how hard you push yourself, or how laser focused you are. There's literally no event in the world that can even come close to the experience of the Olympic Games. I guess that's why people want it so badly and train so hard. But with all of the time I had spent daydreaming about becoming an Olympian, the actuality was far different than my childhood imaginings. The truth is I had only ever fantasized about what I saw on television; the lights and banners at the opening ceremony, the finely-tuned robust athletes competing for their countries, and of course the medals. But for me, there was a lot more to the Olympics than what you get to watch on TV.

Making the team was an absolute dream and a total and complete whirlwind. My mom had flown to Omaha for the trials and was in the stadium when I qualified for the 400 IM. But after the race, there are warm-downs, followed by drug testing, and then interviews with the media. So while I didn't get to see my mom that night, as soon as I got back to my hotel room I called her. "Mom!" I was so excited I could barely speak. "Can I get a tattoo of the Olympic rings?" I was still 15 and I knew I would need her permission, and for some reason, that was the first thing that popped into my mind.

She laughed, "I don't know. We'll have to talk to Dad." Then she went on and on about how proud of me she was. It meant so much to me to have her there, cheering me on the night that I officially made the USA Olympic Team. I was also incredibly thankful that she'd be there when it was time to swim my 200 backstroke. My dad and Danny had stayed home and watched the trials at the Willows, a small restaurant and bar right near my house, with a big hometown crowd, and as soon as I hung up with my mom, I called them. My dad was yelling so loudly into the phone that I could barely make out a word he said. Then I heard Danny's voice on the line. "We're going to China!" My entire life my family had been such a huge support for me, and it brought me to tears knowing how happy they were to see me live out my dream. I knew my parents had sacrificed a lot to make sure I had every opportunity possible to reach my potential, and that night, I couldn't have been more grateful.

The rest of the meet was a daze. But four days later, I also qualified for the Olympic Team in the 200 backstroke, the only event in which I had expected to make it. Once the meet was over and the team had been finalized, the official 2008 USA Olympic Swim Team was paraded out into The Qwest Center to greet a screaming crowd. There was one girl in the lineup who I noticed immediately, Allison Schmitt. I had seen her race, and she qualified for the Olympics in the 200 freestyle. At 18, she was the second youngest person on the team, which made me automatically feel connected to her. Her poofy, curly brown hair was just like mine and she was six foot one. She had the most infectious laugh I've ever heard, and we hit it off right away. Standing in line, decked out in USA gear, about to be announced, we kept staring at each other in awe of what was happening. "Are we really here?" she whispered.

"I know!" We were on the same team as Michael Phelps, Ryan Lochte, Natalie Coughlin, and Katie Hoff. Both of us were giddy with disbelief and beyond thrilled to be a part of the moment we were in. We became fast friends, and it was a relief to have someone on the team who I felt comfortable with. In fact, Schmitty (which was what everyone actually called her) was extremely outgoing. So much so that she helped coax me out of my shell around the rest of the older swimmers. I had been so young when I first made the National Team that I had become accustomed to keeping my head down and spending time on my own. But with Schmitty by my side, some familiar faces, and additional races under my belt, I felt more like a member of the team and less like an outsider.

When you pack for the Olympic trials, you also pack for the Olympics. Once Trials were over, the entire team traveled together to Palo Alto, California for a week long training camp. Then we headed to Singapore and had a two-week training camp at the Singapore Country Club. Unlike in the past, I enjoyed all parts of this camp; the pool, the novelty of our location, and even the time that I got to spend bonding with my team members outside of practice. I was assigned to the national coach, Gregg Troy, who I had worked with before. I loved swimming for someone who was so knowledgeable about the sport and had such an outstanding reputation. Coach Troy was also very close with Chuck, and he would often relay messages from Chuck about my times and splits in practice. I missed training with Chuck, but Coach Troy softened that by always keeping him in the loop. Ryan Lochte was in my lane just like at Pan Pacs training camp, and he was starting to feel less like an unapproachable superstar and more like a big brother. Margaret Hoelzer and Katie Hoff were also becoming good friends, and I looked forward to spending time with them. And of course, there was my new partner in crime, Schmitty. Because Schmitty was a freestyler she trained with another coach, but we spent our off time together, and it was nice that because we had different specializations we weren't ever in competition with one another. The two weeks at camp flew by, and before I knew it the USA Swim Team—swimmers, coaches, staff and all, were being loaded onto a private jet to take us to Beijing.

When we were in the air, I was beside myself. I had never been on a private jet before. Sit wherever you want? Awesome. There were hors d'oeuvres everywhere and the fact that we were on our way to the Olympics made the entire plane ride that much more magical. I had just spent two weeks training at a country club with the best swimmers in the nation, many of whom were expected to medal that year, and now I was munching on cheese and crackers, flying privately somewhere over China. Life was good. Schmitty and I kept smiling at each other, wondering how did we get so lucky? Then we landed. Michael Phelps, one of the greatest Olympians of all time, and my teammate for the 2008 Olympics, was going for a world record eight gold medals in one Olympics which had never been done before. This made him one of the most sought after athletes when it came to the media, and from the moment our plane touched down we were surrounded by paparazzi. In addition to the men with large cameras and blinding flashes, we were hit by a carpet of humidity and smog, and the second we hit the ground everyone was given masks to put over their face because the air quality was so poor. The airport was filled with people speaking a language I didn't understand, and it was a far cry from the ambiance of the Singapore Country Club or the private jet.

After we went through customs, we boarded a bus that had been hired to transfer us to the Olympic Village. Michael ended up sitting across from me, and I could see paparazzi literally pushing up against the window next to him desperately trying to get a decent shot. I sat there, a mask over my face, feeling frazzled. I couldn't wait to get to the Olympic Village. This was the part you didn't get to see on TV, and I pictured plush carpets, big comfy beds, cloth robes, and anything else you would expect from a standard Western hotel. We were at the most exclusive competition in the world, and I assumed that would come with the luxuries I had experienced in Singapore and on the private jet to Beijing. However, when we arrived at the Olympic Village, my accommodation was not what I had expected. The room was barren. There was one tiny bed with a single sheet on it and one pillow, the windows had no curtains, the shower rested over the toilet, and there was nothing to block the shower nozzle from spilling water out in all directions once you turned it on. After we put down our things, we had to get our credentials, and then we headed to a team meeting with the nutritionists from the USA Olympic Team.

I sat down very seriously, ready to take notes on what our diet should consist of in order to reach peak performance in our events. "Alright, so we've been here for a couple of days and have been surveying the food. We strongly recommend that if you want to eat in the Olympic Village you stick to McDonald's." What? At first, I thought it was joke. But they went on. "It's the only place where we know exactly what's in the food. Therefore, the McDonald's in the village is where we suggest that you eat." I was shocked. There I was at the pinnacle of my sport, and I was going to be sleeping on a bed that looked less comfortable than the ground and loading up on fast food. Already, I was uncertain of how anyone would put up their best performance under those circumstances.

Lastly, we went to a meeting with our head coach. Again, I was anticipating some serious strategic talk, but for the most part, it was a lecture on safe sex. It was hard to miss the piles of condoms strategically placed throughout all of the dining halls and set out on every floor of our apartments. But hearing about using protection if we chose to partake in intercourse really threw me for a loop. At 15, I had no idea what to make of that first day at the Olympic Village. And just as I was trying to sort through everything, we were reminded of the real kicker. NBC wanted to air all of the races live during primetime in the United States, which meant that we would be swimming preliminaries at night and finals in the morning, the opposite of how we usually competed. That setup was unheard of, and I had never done a meet like it before. By the end of that afternoon, my head was spinning. To complicate things even more, the 400 IM was the first day of competition. The opening ceremony was two nights away, but attending wasn't even an option for me. I would easily be on my feet until 3 a.m. if I went, and that would leave me in no shape for my race. A few days later as the opening ceremony of the 2008 Beijing Olympic Games began, I settled into my room and tried to organize my thoughts.

The next morning I woke up insanely nervous and overwhelmed.

It was the first day of the Olympic Games, and my race was that night. Not only was I used to swimming preliminaries in the morning, but being the first women's race of the meet, we were expected to set the tone for our teammates. Katie Hoff had also qualified in the 400 IM, so what we did when we went off the blocks mattered—not only to hopefully medal, but to set a precedent that would motivate the other swimmers. If we did great, we started the meet off on the right foot. If we didn't, well, I couldn't even think about that. My mom and Danny had flown to China for the Olympics, and they would be watching from the stands. We couldn't afford for everyone to go, so my dad stayed home and would be watching the race from the Willows, with friends, family, other Rhode Islanders, and NBC. For most states, I guess it wouldn't have been such a big deal that I made the Olympics. But I was the first Olympic swimmer from Rhode Island since 1948, and I knew that everyone back home was cheering for me. Leading up to trials, I had been on the cover of every newspaper in the state, appeared on every news station, and there was even a billboard with my picture wishing me good luck. Not only was I representing the USA and swimming the first day in the first women's race of the meet, I had thousands of people back in Rhode Island rooting for me, and I didn't want to let them down.

From the second I opened my eyes my phone was going off. "Good luck!" "We're all cheering for you!" "Everyone's thinking about you!" "Just saw your billboard on the highway." Shaking my head, I knew everyone just wanted to be encouraging. But with every text I felt more pressure, and thoughts of what could go wrong started creeping through my head. If I thought not qualifying for finals at World Championships was bad, this would be immensely worse. Not only would I be letting down my country, my state, my coaches, my family, and my friends, I would literally be failing while the entire world watched. I eventually had to switch off my phone because I was getting too distracted and since preliminaries weren't until that evening, I spent the entire morning and afternoon pacing and stressing out over my race. That day seemed like a month, and I was relieved when I finally arrived at the pool for prelims. I warmed up like normal, then went to the bathroom and threw up as was becoming routine when I couldn't handle my nerves before a big race. I made it to the ready room just in time, walked out onto the pool deck with my heat, dove in when the beep sounded, and put up the best time of the night. I don't know how I did it, but at 15 years old I was going into finals as the fastest swimmer in the world in my race. The fastest in the world. Needless to say, I barely slept at all. If I was going in seeded first, I had to at least medal, if not win. This was what I had trained for and this is where everything I had worked so hard for came into play. Tossing and turning in my tiny bed, I knew I had to find a way to wrangle in my anxiety and do my best to win.

The next day I was up early, my stomach still in knots just thinking about my event that morning. I went to the dining hall and was relieved to see Ryan. We were both training with Coach Troy so we were on the same schedule, and he was also swimming the 400 IM in finals. I was thankful to see a familiar face and glad for the company. I watched him scarf down three egg McMuffins while I could barely force myself to eat more than a few bites of my yogurt parfait. Ryan glanced up at me. "Hey Beisel, are you okay?" he asked eying my mostly untouched breakfast. I wanted more than anything to be strong and not let him see how terrified I actually was, but I couldn't stop my head from spinning. I was about to perform in front of the whole world, and I didn't know if I was ready. I glanced down at my phone, more messages. "GO USA!" "You've got this." "There are already 500 people at the Willows to watch your race!"

That day I decided to confide in Ryan for the first time but certainly not the last. He was a seasoned competitor, and I was about to crawl out of my skin. "No! I'm not okay. Not at all. Ryan, I'm not sure I can do this."

In a split second, Ryan moved over to my side of the table and had his arm around me. "Look, Beisel. This is your first Olympics!

Do you know how cool that is? All you can do is go out there and do your best. No matter what happens, you have already made it this far. You're so much stronger than you know. I promise, this is going to be your first of many Olympics. Use today as a test run for your future and just go for it!"

It hadn't occurred to me that Ryan might be right and after his pep talk, I was still nervous, but I was also excited. The Olympics had been my dream, and there I was sitting with Ryan about to swim against the best swimmers in the world. Maybe this was just the beginning.

I threw my cell in my bag, and we made our way to the pool. We jumped in for warm-ups and it felt amazing to be back in the water. I tried to focus on my breathing and my strokes and forget about what was at stake. Then I got out, and we were told that President Bush was in the stands and would be watching us swim. You've got to be kidding me. Not only was I about to swim in front of the entire world, but the president was right there in that very building, watching me represent the United States of America.

I was standing where I had always imagined—at the Olympic Games, and the magnitude of that realization was both exhilarating and terrifying. I tried to take a deep breath and shake out my arms. In the minutes leading up to that swim, I had never been more nervous. Once I was announced, all I could do was take my place. Trying to remind myself that I was seeded first, I took my mark with the rest of the swimmers and fired off the block when I heard the beep. Although in IMs it's common for swimmers to exchange positions throughout the different stroke transitions, I started off third and held that position for the duration of the race. I could see the girl in first who held onto a solid lead, and I stuck right behind Katie, who was in second. During the last leg of freestyle, I realized that the girl beside me was beginning to gain ground and I knew that the finish would be close. Summoning all of my strength, I pushed myself as hard as I could, held onto my third place spot and finished right after Katie hit the wall. I was elated. I had just won a bronze medal at the Olympic Games! I glanced up and looked for my name on the scoreboard only to see the number four. The whole race I had been in fourth, not third. There was a swimmer in lane eight outside of my line of sight who got second, Katie got third, and I had just missed a medal by less than a second. There is nothing worse than getting fourth at the Olympic Games.

Climbing out of the pool, I had never been more disappointed. Not only did I feel like a complete failure, but I had missed a medal by so little that it hurt to think about what might have happened if I had gotten off the block a tenth of a second faster, pulled just a little bit stronger, or kicked harder. That wasn't how I had wanted to start my first Olympic Games, but the one consolation was that Katie got third. I went over and gave her an enormous hug. I had learned a lot from watching Katie, not the very least of which was how graceful she was under pressure. I was fully aware that was something I still needed to master, and as difficult as it was to put that loss behind me, I knew I had to let it go and focus on the 200 backstroke. That night I got on the phone with Chuck. "Look," he said. "You're a 15-year-old at the Olympic Games which means you've got nothing to lose. You just got fourth place! Fourth in the world! Think about that. You didn't have to win a medal to prove that you belong there. Just get out there and go for it!"

I knew he was right, so I tried my best to shake off everything; the small room, the diet which solely consisted of McDonald's food, my fourth place finish in the IM, and the expectations of everyone, myself included. I still had a chance to redeem myself, and I hadn't left empty handed yet.

There was still a possibility that I could medal, and the 200 backstroke was by far my strongest event. I pulled myself together and got first place in prelims. When semifinals came, I was once again in first, and I had managed not to throw up before either race which was a victory in itself. But once again, the idea of going into finals as the swimmer with the top time started to get in my head. If I had the first place time entering the race, how would it look if I didn't even medal again? I wasn't expected to qualify for the 400 IM, but the backstroke was my event. Before the 200 backstroke finals, I found myself in the bathroom throwing up in the toilet, and I knew I had started to over-think everything. All the what-ifs began gathering in my brain and by the time I walked out for my race, my entire body felt off and I had lost my focus. I swam my race and got fifth. Glancing up at the scoreboard after I hit the wall, my heart dropped. The 200 backstroke was where I was my very best, and I had done even worse than I had in the 400 IM. The thing that really killed me, looking at the times, was that if I had swum the time I did in trials, I would have gotten second. It wasn't that I did my best and I wasn't able to medal, it was that I hadn't been able to deliver when it mattered most. Before I even got out of the pool in Beijing, I made myself a promise. I would go to London in 2012, and I would medal.

CHAPTER EIGHT

The 2008 Beijing Olympics taught me many things. Mostly to expect the unexpected, and my performance in the 200 backstroke showed me the value of mental preparedness. World Championships had imparted the importance of dedication when it came to physical training, but I had still come in fifth in a race when I realistically could have medaled. At the time, that was a hard reality to swallow, but looking back, each failure I endured during my swimming career was invaluable. Not qualifying for finals at the World Championships had pushed me to a new degree of commitment to my sport that never would have resulted from a feel-good win. Just like coming within a second of a bronze medal in the 400 IM and tanking on the 200 backstroke made me more motivated than ever to go home, train harder, and return better. Those setbacks were painful, sometimes excruciatingly so, but they also gave me the launching pad I needed in order to propel myself to the next level.

After such a huge disappointment, I sulked my way around the Olympic Village. However, because of safety concerns the United States Olympic Committee had decided that all athletes who were 18 and under would leave as soon as their events were over. This made my first Olympics a quick trip. While I was bummed with how I had swum and I wished I could have done better, my only thought leaving Beijing was that in four years I could rewrite my story. I would use that time to become the athlete I knew I was capable of being, and more than I felt defeated, I was intent on improving. I never thought about giving up or throwing away my dream of winning an Olympic medal—that was a goal I had ingrained in myself. So it didn't matter how hard it was or how many times I failed, no matter what I had to keep trying.

As I organized my luggage and all of my Team USA gear, I thought harder about the 2012 London Olympics. The entire trip from trials through to the competition had been one big, crazy, exciting blur and while I was sad to leave, I was also ready to go home. I needed to digest what had happened, and I was beyond happy when I realized that Schmitty and I would be leaving together on the same flight back to the United States. It's difficult to explain the kind of pressure that comes with the Olympics, it's even harder to try and put into words what a failure you feel like when you let down what seems like millions and millions of people. But no one understood what I was going through more than Schmitty. She had come in ninth in the semi-finals of the 200 free, which meant she hadn't made it to finals in the one individual event she had qualified for. And just like me, if she had swum one of the times she had put up in trials, she not only would have made the finals, but she likely could have medaled.

I wasn't sure what type of mood she'd be in the day we flew out, but the first words out of her mouth were "Happy Birthday!" We were flying home on my 16th birthday, and I laughed. After the Olympics and everything that had happened since trials, my birthday didn't seem like that big of a deal. "You know what's really cool?" she asked.

I shook my head.

"We're going to be traveling in different time zones, so your birthday's going to be like 36 hours long!"

"I hadn't thought of that."

Despite that I was still down and a little shell-shocked from the whole experience, I immediately felt better once I was with Schmitty. She has always been the type of person who can make anyone's day better, and I appreciated her enthusiasm. And if there was one thing she was right about, it was that my birthday and our flight did seem to last forever. However, I couldn't have been more grateful that we had those hours sitting in the sky, uninterrupted, together. Both of us knew we had blown our races, but instead of beating ourselves up, we started encouraging each other. It was about halfway through our flight when I stared out the window and nervously bit my lip. There was something I wanted say to Schmitty, but for some reason it felt almost too huge to voice aloud. "You know what would be really cool?" I finally asked.

"If we hadn't lost!" Schmitty replied.

I rolled my eyes and laughed. "Well, yeah. But," I leaned in closer. "If we come back in four years and win gold medals together!"

Schmitty's face instantly lit up and she was grinning from ear to ear. For a moment neither of us said anything, there was a palpable rush of emotion and I knew from Schmitty's expression that she was in. "I really think we can do it."

"I know we can."

We were young, we were capable of swimming times that could have medaled, and this was both of our first Olympics. We were the only two 18 and under swimmers on the USA Olympic Team, and there was no way we weren't going to return more experienced, faster, stronger, and better prepared. We weren't just coming back; we were coming back with a vengeance. We shared the same unrelenting determination and talking to each other about what we wanted to accomplish only ignited that natural competitive drive. By the time our flight landed, we had already mapped out our assault on the London 2012 Olympics. When it came time for the next Olympic Games, we would show up and swim the best times of our lives. I knew after that trip, I had a made a lifelong friend.

It was hard to part ways with Schmitty once we made it back to the States, but it went without saying that we would stay in touch. As she boarded her flight home to Detroit, I caught my plane to Providence. Flying back to Rhode Island, there were so many thoughts racing through my mind that I stopped trying to make sense of them. Absolutely exhausted after traveling for over 30 some hours, the last few weeks were beginning to feel like a daze. I was just glad that my dad was picking me up at the airport. I couldn't wait to see him, and I was already imagining how amazing it would feel to crawl into my own bed. Getting off the plane, I drug my feet towards baggage claim, and tried to keep my eyes open. I was so tired I almost tripped when I got on the escalator, and then I looked up. There was a mass of over 100 people waiting down below, and as soon as they saw me everyone started cheering. My jaw dropped. There were friends, family members, news stations, and people who I didn't even recognize. There were posters that said "Happy Birthday," "Congratulations," and "Welcome Home, Elizabeth!" It took a moment to register that everyone was there for me. I was blown away.

As soon as I got to the bottom of the escalator, I had eight microphones in my face. "What did you think about the Olympics?" "Were you happy with your performance?" "How did you feel about the competition?" "Are you glad to be home?"

I was speechless. The questions they were asking me, I hadn't even had a chance to ask myself. I didn't know how to respond or what to say. I was overwhelmed, moved, completely caught off guard, and touched beyond words to realize that people actually cared that much. I knew making the Olympics was a big deal to me, and I had gotten the texts, and seen the newspaper articles, and even heard about the billboard with my face on it, but I hadn't believed it was that big of a deal to other people until I saw the crowd there that night. I realized then, even though I hadn't medaled, I had done something special. Looking at everyone who had gathered there to welcome me home, I thought that maybe making the team was good for Rhode Island. What I had accomplished might actually have brought people together and given them something to cheer for, even if it had only lasted for a few weeks. That recognition shook me to my core.

That night was fantastic, but I'd be lying if I said adjusting to life as "the Olympic swimmer girl" was easy. I had always been a phenomenal swimmer. It's just that not everyone knew about it. I had broken records since I was seven, so it wasn't news to me that

I was fast. But suddenly, to everyone else, swimming was what defined me. I thought making the Olympic Games was going to be life changing in regards to accomplishing my own goals, but I didn't realize that my entire world would be different when I got home. That wasn't part of what the little girl watching the Sydney Games had anticipated when I had set my sights on being an Olympian. But it was my reality.

I had sponsorship deals coming in from all over the place, people wanted to name car dealerships and food items on menus after me, and I was on the cover of every newspaper in Rhode Island. There were people who tried to get me to sign with an agent, go professional, and forfeit my NCAA eligibility before I had even gotten my driver's license. Thankfully my parents were incredibly grounded, and refused to get caught up in any of it. I was going to high school just like everyone else my own age, and they treated me the same as they always had. Instead of feeling overshadowed, as I'm sure a lot of siblings would, Danny made it known how proud he was that I was his sister. He even saved newspaper clippings and media coverage of my Olympic journey and hung them up on his wall. When everything else in my life seemed completely chaotic, my family was my rock and no matter how crazy things got, home was always my refuge.

At school, people who I didn't know suddenly wanted to be my best friend, and even the teachers wanted my autograph. Before I had been the girl who won local swim meets, but now it seemed like everyone wanted a piece of me. I went from having a few close friends to being crowned Prom Queen, getting invitations to every party, and having people stare at me wherever I went. I would go to the grocery store or Walmart and numerous people would stop and ask me to take a photograph with them. At that point, I still couldn't even drive so my parents became my unofficial photographers. It was a given when we went out in public that people would ask me to pose with them, and after a while my mom and dad automatically just started grabbing their cameras once they approached us.

When I was walking through the hallways at high school, I quickly grew used to hearing people mumble under their breath as I passed. "There's the Olympic swimmer girl," kids would say in whispers loud enough that I couldn't not hear. Other students would take my picture when I was at my locker, and one of my teachers posted a front page newspaper story about me on the chalkboard, complete with my signature, that hung directly in front of me as I tried to concentrate during class.

A few months later, I was at the State Championships swim meet for my high school. I had looked at the meet as an opportunity to earn some points for my team and spend some much needed time with my friends. Riding the bus to the meet, I actually felt a rejuvenating sense of normalcy. It was great to be doing what everyone else was doing for a change. But when we got to the meet, I was bombarded with people who wanted to take pictures with me and get my autograph. I was overwhelmed, and barely able to spend any time hanging out with my teammates as I had hoped. When I went up to the blocks for my race, the crowd didn't let up. There was line of people behind me waiting with cameras and pens, and finally I had to turn around. "I'm sorry." I felt awful telling people no. "But I can't sign your cap or take a photo right now." I gestured to the pool. "I'm swimming in 30 seconds. I'll get you after." In the end, I almost missed one of my races because all of the distractions.

Once I got out of the pool, I went into the locker room to change. I needed some space and wanted a minute to myself. As soon as I had locked myself in a dressing room, I heard a group of girls enter. "What does she think she's doing here?"

"She just went to the freaking Olympics, give somebody else a chance to win. What's her problem?"

"Obviously she just loves the attention and could care less about anybody else."

"I don't get what the big deal about her is anyways."

They never said my name, and they didn't have to. I didn't know them, they didn't know me, and they had no idea that I could hear what they were saying. But none of that stopped their words from being hurtful. I had been optimistic that once the buzz of the Olympics died down, everything would go back to normal. All I wanted to do was fit in. But that day, sitting there with my head down in the locker room long after those girls left, I realized things might not ever return to how they had been before. In hindsight, I wouldn't do anything differently, but it took some time for it to sink in that my life wouldn't ever be the same.

CHAPTER NINE

The attention never faded away entirely, but eventually I got more used to dealing with random people asking for my picture and recognizing me when I was out and about and once again started focusing on my training. By that point, swimming had easily become my biggest priority, along with school, and I continued to improve as I trained at Bluefish with Chuck. It wasn't that I loved violin any less or that I didn't want to hang out with my friends, but 99 percent of the time, when I had a choice, I chose swimming. It was what I loved, and once I made the decision that I wanted to be the best, I backed that up with as much dedication and hard work as I could physically and mentally manage.

That summer I qualified for the 2009 World Championships in the 400 IM and the 200 back, just like I had at the Olympics. But this time I was thrilled to learn that Chuck would be joining me as a coach at the Championships, which would be held in Rome, Italy. I had started to make a real name for myself in swimming, and that's why Chuck was asked to be a coach as opposed to meets in the past when I trained with other national coaches during international meets. Chuck and I had ironed out a training routine that worked, and he honed in on the various nuances that got me to my best when it came to the pool. Our disagreements were a thing of the past, and I found myself constantly thinking about how grateful I was that he came into my life. He sacrificed everything for his athletes, and our partnership as an athlete and coach meant the world to me. That meet, I received my first medal for Team USA which was monumental. For so long, I had attended those meets and hoped beyond hope that I would be taking home a medal and placing third in the 200 backstroke and getting the bronze only fueled my desire to improve. I finally made the podium for my country, and I had Chuck by my side while doing it. It was by far one of my greatest accomplishments.

When I returned home, I said goodbye to Laura, who had remained one of my best friends throughout everything. Once she left for college it was difficult to imagine what swimming at Bluefish would be like without her. She had decided to swim for the University of Texas, and her decision made me think about my own future when it came to swimming. Because of strict NCAA rules, colleges cannot recruit athletes until July 1 before their senior year of high school. Which I didn't think was a big deal until that date hit. I was the only high school swimmer who had competed in the Olympics and I had phone calls, voicemails, and letters from every university I had ever even considered attending offering me full scholarships.

After the Beijing Olympics, I had kept in touch with Schmitty who was now swimming for the University of Georgia, and hearing about Schmitty and Laura's experiences on their college teams made me excited to start visiting campuses and begin trying to decide where I wanted to go. I missed Laura when practice at Bluefish revved up again, but I quickly became close with Anna Senko during my senior year, who was a new addition to the team. We both swam the 200 backstroke and 400 IM, so we were automatically training partners. She pushed me in practice just as much as Laura did, and she had the most positive outlook on life of anyone I knew. She was one of the fastest seniors in the country as well, and we went through the college recruiting procedure together. There was a lot to maneuver when it came to selecting the right school to swim for, and having someone to go through that process with made it much more manageable and fun. We instantly became best friends and spent hours upon hours discussing schools we wanted, schools we thought we might want, and schools we knew we didn't want. We leaned on each other when we got frustrated and were also able to cheer each other on when we made strides towards figuring things out.

In addition to having Anna as a sounding board, I talked to my parents and Danny, Schmitty and Laura, and numerous coaches endlessly when I was trying to make my final list of universities. In the end, I narrowed my list of schools down to three; the University of Florida, the University of Texas, and the University of California, Berkeley. All three had various pros and I had no idea how I would choose between them. I considered the University of Florida because Gregg Troy coached there and not only was their program legendary, but I had loved working with him at Pan Pacs, World Championships, and the Olympics. The University of Texas also had a competitive team, and I was drawn there because I could train with Laura, who was thriving in her new surroundings. And the University of California, Berkeley was a no-brainer as the number one ranked public school in the nation with one of the top swimming programs in the country as well.

With my senior year of high school, training six days a week, and researching colleges, I had a lot on my plate. But visiting each of my top three schools on recruiting trips only made me that much more eager to begin my journey as a college swimmer. Everywhere I went I got to go to football games, tour the dorms, meet swimmers from the team, and sit down with each and every head coach individually to discuss what the next four years might look like if I chose their school. All of the universities had stellar swim programs, impressive academics, gorgeous campuses, and welcoming teams. But ultimately, my decision boiled down to the conversation I had with Coach Troy when I visited the University of Florida. Gregg Troy was not only known for coaching Ryan Lochte, but also for leading the University of Florida swim program to their elite reputation. Olympians and world record holders from all over the world wanted to go to the University of Florida so that they could swim under Coach Troy, and he fostered an Olympic culture which was embedded in the University of Florida's swim team. He was also known for running a grueling and demanding training program, but that was what I wanted.

I still remember sitting down with Coach Troy once I had toured the University of Florida. I was already comfortable in his presence from the amount of time I had spent training with him, and I was anxious to hear his thoughts on what my future may hold. I was expecting a long conversation about my goals and dreams and what kind of training mentality he required of his swimmers. Instead, he asked me one question with a subtle confidence that I couldn't help but be impressed by. "Do you want to be an Olympic champion?" he posed the question so straightforwardly that for a moment I was taken aback.

"Of course, I do." That's what I had wanted since I was seven years old, and sitting there in his office, I was more invested in that goal than ever.

"Then you should come to Florida." After that one sentence, I knew what my decision would be. I committed to the University of Florida and couldn't wait to call Schmitty, Laura, and Anna (who had just committed to swim at UCLA the week before) to tell them the news. When I called Anna we both squealed in delight that we had reached the end of the recruiting stint and found schools we were enthusiastic about. Laura was thrilled for me and told me that the University of Florida was a great choice, and Schmitty was pumped. Not only would we be geographically closer but the University of Georgia was in the same conference as the University of Florida, which meant we would see one another at swim meets on a regular basis. My parents and Danny supported my decision wholeheartedly, and even the coach at the University of California, Berkeley graciously wished me the best of luck and told me she knew I would do phenomenally well at Florida and in my future. Everything about the University of Florida seemed to fit, and I couldn't wait to swim for Coach Troy, take my training to the next level, and enjoy warm sunny winters in the South. But as with all change, even such a positive milestone was still bittersweet at times.

As I finished my senior year of high school, I knew that my life was about to shift enormously. I had never lived outside of Rhode Island, and as excited as I was for Florida, I knew that I would miss my friends and family at home immensely. Not only would I have to leave behind my friends and family, I'd be graduating from Bluefish Swim Club, which had become just as much my home as Rhode Island. Chuck and I had inarguably gotten off to a rocky start, but we had cemented our relationship over the years, and I trusted him and questioned whether another coach would be capable of picking up where he would leave off. Just like when Josh had left and Carl had been assigned to another group of swimmers, part of me wondered if there would be anyone else who could ever take their place. I suppose the answer was that there wasn't. And there wasn't anyone capable of taking Chuck's place either. Every coach has their own style, their own way of connecting with their athletes, and their individual philosophy when it comes to what works both in and out of the pool. And although I felt in my gut that I had made the right decision committing to Florida and to Coach Troy, the transition was still a big one.

After high school graduation, I attended Nationals and qualified again for the Pan Pacific Championships which would be my last meet with Chuck as my coach. Ironically, both Nationals and Pan Pacs were held in Irvine that year, at the very same pool where I had gone to my first Nationals with Chuck and qualified for my first USA National Team. Although only four years had passed, I had grown tremendously during that time. It was humbling to be back to where I had first officially started swimming for Team USA, and it was emotional to know from that day forward my swimming career with Chuck would be over. The worst part was that Pan Pacs took place during the first week of school at the University of Florida. So on top of all of the emotional pulls that came with the upheaval of change, I was missing out on the first week of classes with all of the other freshmen. Being the best was still what I wanted more than anything, but there were times when that seemed to cost a lot. Sitting by the pool, surrounded by world class swimmers, the only thing that seemed absolute was my uncertainty.

During training camp before Pan Pacs, even though I had been on a solid streak of successfully wrangling in my often stubborn nerves, I couldn't get out of my own head. I was worried that everyone at the University of Florida was making friends, breaking off into groups, and having the most amazing time of their lives, and that I'd missed out on my opportunity to be a normal college student. It was only a week, but I didn't want to arrive and be the one person who hadn't made any connections. Plus, I didn't know anything about what my training with Coach Troy would really entail. What if I didn't get faster like I was supposed to? What if I didn't get along with the rest of the team? It had taken a long time before Chuck and I had broken into a comfortable training stride, and it felt like I was giving all that up and starting over. My thoughts kept weighing me down and circling aimlessly in my mind, which was distracting and I was swimming terribly. After a few days of not performing in sets that should have been easy, I was frustrated and starting to worry about what my times would be at the meet. One afternoon after a grinding 400 IM set that I swam horribly, Coach Troy pulled me out of the water. "Talk to me," he said.

I didn't even know where to begin. My entire life was transforming right before my eyes, and it didn't matter that all of what I was going through was a necessary transition. I couldn't focus on anything other than the apprehension that pulsed within. "I don't know how I can be expected to be the best in the world in one week if I'm swimming the worst times I've swum in months."

"It's not always about the practice."

"What do you mean?" I asked.

"Listen," he said knowingly. "There are two types of swimmers. There are racers and there are pacers. Pacers can throw down great times consistently in practice, but they never go much faster in the meet itself. Racers are a different breed. Pacing, you can teach. But you either know how to race or you don't. When you're a racer, once you get on that block, all bets are off. Pacers are more predictable, but if you can race, that changes the game entirely when it's time to compete. Your pacing has been off. But that doesn't matter. You're a racer. Next week, you just have to step up onto that block and do what you do best."

I wasn't sure what to say, so I simply nodded. It was similar to when Josh had gently lectured me on the importance of weaknesses or when Nelson waved his gold medal in my face at trials and told me to believe in myself. It's not always the times you expect that are most defining, it's often the fortuitous moments when something as simple as a well-spoken thought can rock your entire world. What Coach Troy said made sense, and if he was right I had nothing to worry about at Pan Pacs. So I got back in the pool, started swimming again, and silently prayed that he knew what he was talking about when it came to me being a racer.

Almost immediately I was able to pluck myself out of my dizzying spell of downward thinking and focus on Pan Pacs. I was still bummed that I had to skip my first week at the University of Florida. I didn't want to miss out on bonding with my classmates because I was in California while they were all moving into their dorms, going to parties, and making lifelong friendships. But when I was in our team room, I found myself next to Teresa Crippen. Teresa had been my host when I visited the University of Florida the year before, and she was solidifying herself as one of the top butterfliers in the world. She was also one of the hardest workers I had ever met, and would be one of my training partners at the University of Florida. She was two years ahead of me in school, but she seemed 10 years more mature and knowledgeable. "Hey!"

"Hey, Teresa."

"How's the training going? I'm so glad you're going to be at Florida this year."

I sighed. "Yeah. It's going okay. Florida will be good," I replied, a little too unenthusiastically.

"What's wrong?"

"Nothing. It's just the thought of swimming for a brand new coach. I've gotten so used to Chuck, and he knows my strokes and how I work best. The idea of swimming for someone else seems crazy. I mean, what if I can't perform for Coach Troy the same way I do for Chuck? What if it doesn't work? Or Florida's not a good fit?"

Teresa sat back patiently. "It's going to be fine. Trust me. Coach Troy's an amazing coach. And yes, it's going to be different, and I'm going to warn you now—it's going to be hard. But it will be absolutely worth it. If you do what Coach Troy says and work hard, it will pay off in the end."

Still uncertain, I shook my head. "I can't believe I'm missing the first week of school for this. I feel like everyone's going to have gotten to know each other and I'll have missed out on everything. The last thing I want is to start college with no friends because I got there a week late."

That time, Teresa couldn't help but laugh. "I promise you, it's not that big of a deal. You'll have plenty of time to make friends. The first week isn't all it's cracked up to be. The only things you're going to miss are a bunch of boring presentations. UF is awesome, and you'll love it. Besides, you're not going in without any friends," she said with a large smile. "You've got me."

After speaking with Teresa and getting my pep talk from Coach Troy, I was able to breathe a huge sigh of relief. Leaving Rhode Island was scary. There was no getting around that. And moving beyond Bluefish and Chuck and continuing my swimming career at college was what the future is for everyone, a reality that offered no steadfast guarantees. But it was such a godsend that I had two incredible people willing to encourage me who would be part of my new life as a Gator at the University of Florida. So once Pan Pacs began, I knew I had to listen to Coach Troy, suck it up, and dive off the blocks and race.

Looking around before my events, I realized how at ease I had felt within a place that used to be so foreign. That first meet in Irvine when I had made the National Team, I had barely had the courage to leave Chuck's side. I had been the smallest, the youngest, and the least experienced swimmer at the entire meet. Sure, I still had anxieties and apprehensions, but being at such a high profile event felt almost normal. I no longer looked down at the concrete nervously or questioned whether or not I belonged. In the four years since I had qualified for the National Team, I had grown in every way possible. I now looked the part and blended in with the other toned and taut swimmers who stretched by the pool awaiting their heat. I had competed in Canada, Australia, Italy, China, and all over the United States. I had gone to the Olympic Games, and I knew that I had pushed myself as much as possible to be the best swimmer I could be. In doing so not only had I become a better athlete, but I had become a stronger and more resilient person. Joining the USA National Team had been intimidating at the beginning, but it had also opened up so many doors.

Suddenly, the unknown didn't seem quite as frightening or as treacherous. I had faced it before, and I would inevitably face it again. But I was thankful that I could end my swimming career with Chuck at the first place where it had really begun. Chuck had changed me as a swimmer, and I knew I would be indebted to him forever for that. It was truly a full circle moment for me, and despite that I wasn't sure of what lie ahead, I was content knowing that I had given my all when it came to what I was leaving behind.

I no longer questioned where to go or how to stand or even what cap I should be wearing. Navigating my way through the commonalities of a large meet had become second nature and not only did I know what to do and how to handle myself, I had coaches and other swimmers at that level who I knew well, cheering me on. There might have been a lot of things that were still ambiguous, but whether or not I was a swimmer who belonged at that level of competition was no longer a question. Progress is sometimes very slow and gradual, so it can be easy to take how far you've come for granted. But being back in Irvine, I was keyed into how much I had accomplished in the last four years. There were parts of the journey that had been more amazing and life changing than I had imagined, and there were difficulties I had never anticipated. But I was happy with the path I had chosen and wouldn't change a thing.

That week at Pan Pacs when they announced my lane, I walked out with my head held high and listened as the crowd roared. I heard the whistle blow and climbed up onto the block. "Take your mark," the familiar words echoed, and when I heard the beep, I exploded into the water. During that week I swam the 400 IM and the 200 backstroke and won gold in both. Coach Troy was right, I was a racer.

CHAPTER TEN

I had no idea what to expect when it came to the University of Florida. As much as I wanted to start college, moving to new state, joining a new team, and entering into a totally new phase of life was as daunting as it was exhilarating. I couldn't wait to get to Gainesville and begin my career as a Gator, but at the same time, anxiety danced in my stomach at the thought of walking onto the pool deck for the first time. Because it was so difficult for me early on to connect with my teammates, my apprehension about whether or not I would fit in was definitely compounded. I prayed and hoped that it wouldn't be like when I had first joined the national team and found myself eating all my meals alone and retreating to my room as an escape. Generally, joining new teams had been hard so, as confident as I was in my decision, I was still holding my breath to see what the actuality of swimming at the University of Florida would be like.

When I arrived after Pan Pacs, I realized that all of my fears had been irrelevant. The swimmers on the team welcomed me warmly. I was already at ease with Coach Troy because I had trained with him before, and even if I hadn't known him, his reputation would have preceded him. There was no question that he was one of the greatest coaches in the world, and I didn't doubt that he could make me a better swimmer. Ryan Lochte and Teresa Crippen were two familiar faces that immediately made me feel at home, and whether or not I would be able to make friends on the team was no longer a question after the first few practices. My Gator teammates became my new best friends and we leaned on one another as if we were family.

The training was no joke, and if I thought Bluefish was intense, Coach Troy had a whole new level of expectations. I went from swimming once a day to swimming twice a day and adding in dry land training which included running, sit-ups, jumping rope, and boxing. When we did stadium stairs, I came in dead last and could barely lift my legs the next day. I had never done cross training before, and I was physically exhausted. In the weight room, I lifted less than literally every other member of the team. And on top of the increase in training, I was faced with navigating a gigantic campus and keeping up with courses much more vigorous than I had been used to in high school. The new freshmen and I bonded over the strenuous workouts and the challenge of balancing school and practice. There was a lot to take on, but swimming gave me an automatic group of friends and an awesome community where I felt I belonged which made the transition manageable.

Even surrounded by teammates who had quickly become my best friends, there were definitely days when I doubted that I could handle everything. With the amount of training I was doing on a weekly basis, it wasn't atypical to wonder whether or not I was capable of keeping up. But I stuck with it, and I believed what Teresa had said—if I put in the hard work with Coach Troy, it would pay off in the end. Besides, the answer to the one question he had asked me on my visit was still a resounding yes. I wanted to be an Olympic Champion. So no matter how grueling the intervals were or how hard I had to push myself during the dry land workouts, I kept going. It took a while to get used to the amp up in training, but Coach Troy and I had an amazing rapport right from the beginning. I was eager to do what he said, and he was always calling me into his office. "What do you think of the training?" he'd ask, genuinely interested in my feedback. "Is there anything we aren't doing in practice that you'd like me to implement?" Not only did I respect Gregg Troy as a coach, but it meant a lot to me that he asked for my input. He was in constant contact with Chuck, and I knew he was trying to make the shift in training as seamless as possible. That made me even more motivated to give my all in practice.

Teresa was right. That season I worked harder than I had ever worked before; and I also swam the fastest times I had ever swum. All of the hours in the pool, the weights, and what often felt like endless cross-training on dry land had propelled me into phenomenal swimming shape. I could cut through the water more easily, my strength had increased, and my endurance had developed beyond any previous capacity. The final meet of the college season was that March. We went to the 2011 Division 1 NCAA Championships which was held at the University of Texas. From the moment our plane touched down in Austin, I knew it was going to be a good meet. I felt physically better than I ever had, and mentally I was focused. I knew I had come prepared. The hours I had logged at the pool and the days when I could barely make it home from practice weren't easy. Balancing school along with training wasn't always smooth or uncomplicated, but somehow, I had done it. I walked into the NCAA Championships with my teammates, knowing I was ready for the first real test of my collegiate swimming career. The entire team did great, and I swam the fastest times I had ever put up. I ended up being named the 2011 Southeastern Conference Female Freshman swimmer of the year. We did incredible as a team and leaving the NCAA Championships I felt like I was on top of the world.

When I returned to the University of Florida, I was flooded with pride. I had made it through Coach Troy's infamously hard workouts and was swimming my best times ever. I loved my teammates, and I had managed to make straight A's in all of my classes even with the demands of practice. Not only had I made it through my first season of swimming for the University of Florida, I had done so with flying colors. Besides, for once, I wasn't the odd person out. I didn't have to swim with people twice my age who didn't want me in their lane or avert my eyes when everyone else made social plans for after practice. People weren't taking pictures of me when I walked through campus or whispering to their friends about how I had gone to the Olympics. In fact, outside of swim I blended in just like any other college freshman. And I loved it. Once the NCAA Championships were over, I took a long sigh of relief. This was the perfect time for me and my friends to let loose. The first night we were back, I was headed home to my dorm. It was a random Wednesday, and I usually would have studied and gone to bed. "Want to go out?" my friend asked.

Usually I had my typical excuses primed and ready. "Sorry, I can't I have practice." "I wish I could, but I've got swim." "Early morning tomorrow." "Meet next week." At that point I had been a member of Team USA since I was 13 years old. I knew how to dedicate myself to a goal, and I had become very good at saying no. But for some reason, I didn't want to say no anymore. I was in college, I had spent so much time devoted to training for so long, and now I wanted to celebrate. For so many years, I had followed such a strict schedule, and I had politely declined party invitations and offers to go out so often that it was almost automatic—which suddenly made doing the opposite that much more appealing. I heard the word "yes" drop from my lips.

After all of the times I had put swimming first, for once, I wanted to experience life from the perspective of everyone else. I wanted to do a keg stand and stay out until dawn. Everyone else was going out to the bars and throwing back fluorescently toxic looking shots, and I didn't want to be the only one sitting at home going to bed early. In fact, once I started going out, I had such a blast that I kept at it. We had drunken heart-to-hearts on humid Florida nights, and watched the sun rise on our way home. We danced, and drank beer, and sang at the top of our lungs. It felt good to let my hair down and enjoy myself, and it wasn't as if I was skipping class or not making it to practice. I was still showing up. Sure, I was a little less focused and everything seemed to take a lot more effort. But I liked letting go, releasing my inhibitions, and throwing caution to the wind. It seemed like a rite of passage and after all of the hours I had spent at the pool, I felt like I had earned some free time to just have fun.

When I started partying, not only did my sleep habits and alcohol intake change dramatically, but so did what I ate. Although my diet was never perfect, it became horrendous. The day after a night out I'd load up on pizza, cheese sticks, french fries, a big platter of fried food, or whatever they happened to be serving at the dining hall. Junk food actually tasted awesome, who knew? And it was unlimited, all I had to do was swipe my meal plan card and voila. Not to mention that I was always starving with the strenuous training plans and my late nights out. But I didn't think much about it. I had a great time when I went out, my grades didn't suffer, swim was hard but swim was always hard I told myself, and this continued until May. I'd go out three or four times a week, barely sleep, and try to stave off my insatiable appetite with plates of greasy food from the dining hall with next to no nutritional value.

In May we had a long course meet and inexplicably, I went in with the expectation that I'd be able to perform at the level I had in March. No matter what had happened, how big of a funk I had gotten myself into, or how many negative thoughts had roared through my brain before a race, I had almost always still been within the top eight swimmers. Even on my worst days when I had hung my head in despair, I still made what anyone in the swimming world would have deemed a remarkable, top tier time. No, I wasn't always able to pull out a win, but I was always able to make a formidable attempt. So when I warmed up and took my place behind the block, I felt ready. Swimming was what I did, it was what I was good at, and when I hit the water, things usually just made sense. When I dove into the pool and started my race, I knew something was off. Normally I was at the front of the pack, but this time I was nowhere close. Every fiber of my being burned as I tried to push myself to my usual pace, but no matter how hard I tried, my body wouldn't fall in line. My shoulders ached with each movement, my rotation was off, and I was out of breath when I should have been gaining speed. The entire race was a painful struggle, and I was gasping for air by the time I hit the wall.

It was the first time I was ever afraid to look at my time after a race, and I had swum way worse than I had anticipated. Adding a few seconds to my time would have been a major disappointment. But I hadn't added a few seconds, I had added fifteen. Fifteen full seconds to the time I had swum two months ago. I didn't even know that was possible.

When I got out of the pool, I was mortified. If I thought the pressure of going faster than expected was bad or coming in fourth was a nightmare, well, bombing so hard in front of everyone was downright humiliating. I had been putting up stellar times for so long, I didn't realize I was capable of regressing that much, especially in such a short amount of time. I thought that following Coach Troy's workout plan would be enough, and that everything else would naturally take care of itself. My performance shocked me. I was slow. Not slow for me, but really slow. When I found out that I had placed 40th something my jaw dropped. Coach Troy came up to me after the race and I stared down at the floor shamefully.

"Look, it's hard training season so you aren't expected to go your fastest. But Elizabeth, you've got to do the right things," he said.

I looked up at him blankly, uncertain what he meant.

"It's alright. You've just got to stick to the training, and stay with the course. But you've got to do the right things, okay? Do the right things."

I nodded vaguely, still in disbelief. After Coach Troy was done talking to me a senior from my team came over who was a little less discreet. "Hey."

"Hi."

"Rough race."

"Yeah."

Crossing his arms, he caught my eye. "Have you..." he paused for a second. "Have you been taking care of your body these last few months?"

It sounds crazy looking back, but I really hadn't thought about it. "Yeah." I had been swimming at practice and always did the cross training no matter how tired or hungover I was from the night before.

He frowned. "Really?"

"Gosh, I don't know." I let his question sink in. I had been going out more than normal. Okay, a lot more than normal. But everyone went out. And I was eating garbage. But I was working out so much it didn't really matter what I ate. Right?

He shook his head disapprovingly.

"I guess not," I replied. That seemed to be the answer he was fishing for. After our conversation, I made my way back to the locker room. Was that what Coach Troy meant by doing the right things? In the hustle and bustle of college and the pull between trying to be normal and striving to be an Olympian, had I lost the sense of balance I had always been able to find? The more I thought about it, the more certain I was of the answer. Absolutely. Flying home, I couldn't believe that I had gone that far off the rails. What was I thinking? How could I have thought that I could pull all-nighters, drink till last call, cram in studying, and then show up to the pool and put my body through Olympic level training with no consequences? Sitting on the plane, I knew I had messed up. It was my first time on my own, and I had never had that sort of free reign. The season had gone so well, but I had overcompensated on my celebratory endeavors. Sure, I had wanted to know what it felt like not to have to fit my life squarely into the regimented agenda that training required, but not at the expense of being the best. Foolishly, I had thought I could manage both, and I wasn't sure how much damage I had done.

The day after we got back to the University of Florida, I immediately went to the gym and weighed myself. I was 18 pounds heavier than I had been. I cringed as I looked at the scale. That was the wake-up call I needed. I had let things get out of hand, but from that very minute I reeled myself in. No more. Fifteen seconds and 18 pounds was enough. A surge of nausea washed over me, standing in the gym, as I realized that World Championships were six weeks away. I couldn't go to World Championships as some out of shape hot mess. If I continued down this path I probably wouldn't even be able to fit into my racing suit by Worlds. I knew I had to make a change, and just like that, my two months as a Florida party girl came to a screeching halt.

I went to my weights coach first, and he gave me a comprehensive workout program. The next person I went to find was Teresa. She had become like a big sister to me, and I trusted her more than anyone. Once I found her, I told her everything; the late nights, the junk food, the partying, the 15 seconds, and the 18 pounds. "Worlds are coming up. What am I going to do?" I asked with tears in my eyes.

Teresa's usual gentle nature hardened. She pursed her lips in thought and placed her hand on her hip. For a moment, I thought she was going to reprimand me. "Alright, Beisel," she said sternly. "This is the deal. For the next month and a half, we're doing everything together. Do you hear me? You're going to every practice with me. You're eating every meal with me, and we're going to take care of this."

I can't even put into words the gratitude I felt at that moment. Wrapping my arms around her, I agreed. "Thank you. Thank you, so much."

After that day, Teresa took me under her wing and did exactly as she had promised. We ate every meal together, went to every workout together, and she was brilliant. She knew how to eat in order to fuel the correct way—what foods to consume and the proper quantity required. Unlike me, she was used to cardio and weights and knowledgeable about how to maximize the benefits of cross-training without overdoing it. I stuck by her side like glue, and she selflessly and generously encouraged me, cheered me on, and shared everything she knew that would help me get back to where I had been.

That July, I showed up to the 2011 World Championships 18 pounds lighter, and what I hoped would be 15 seconds faster. Worlds were held in Shanghai, China that year at the Shanghai Oriental Sports Center. The stadium was enormous and all of the walls were painted a bright blue that made me feel happy and calm. I had grown fond of the larger venues, and it felt right to be there, about to swim in front of a big crowd. It had taken a lot of practices, early nights, and meal planning, to reclaim my pace times and lose the weight I had gained. But I had continued to do everything Coach Troy asked of me, leaned on Teresa for guidance, and worked myself back to a place where I felt physically and mentally strong. That first year was a huge lesson for me. I took for granted that I had always had the advantage of being healthy, and I knew I had jeopardized my swimming by treating my body so carelessly. But the lesson that came with my mistake was that nutrition and a healthy lifestyle in general were now something I knew how to prioritize. Plus, I liked the way my body felt when I was eating clean, working out hard, and getting the rest I needed.

My two events were the same as always—200 backstroke and 400 IM. The 200 backstroke was up first, and I was pumped. Backstroke was where I had always excelled. With Coach Troy's training, my new healthy eating regime, and dry land conditioning, I was ready to jump in the water, rock that stadium, blow the crowd away, and win my first gold at World Championships. I had done everything right. Well, at least after May, and my hopes were high as I sat in the ready room. First place. I've got this. Instead of working myself into a frenzy or throwing up in the bathroom as I had in my younger years, I sat coolly, confidently. This was my event, and I was going to win. When they announced my name, I walked out like I owned that pool and smiled as the crowd screamed. After a few months off center, I had fought to get back to my best and I was about to dive into the pool and prove it.

Once my feet left the block, my body fell into the familiar rhythm that had taken years to instill and perfect. I moved smoothly, easily, and my strokes were dead on. I almost smiled out of sheer relief that the incident in May was now just a blip. I still had it, and I picked up momentum and gained speed with each turn. When I hit the wall I was pleased with how I had raced, until I saw the results. I had come in fifth place. That wasn't what was supposed to happen. This was my big comeback. I had worked for it. I had battled my way back from flippant party girl to hardcore Olympian, and my big moment was a fifth place finish? It was a frustrating race for me because I knew I had done well, but I still hadn't been able to touch my best time which was from 2008. After three full years, I was still two seconds off, and hitting that time again felt like a brick wall which was impenetrable. I had been so certain that with the last six weeks I would have been able to race that time again or maybe even beat it. But I wasn't even close. Granted, I wasn't 15 seconds slower either, but that time was a memory I wanted to forget.

I couldn't shake the disappointment of the 200 backstroke. It might not have been justified to have set my sights so high, but I had and the more I thought about it, the more I wished I could have done better. What were all the practices and hours and hours spent training for if I couldn't even beat my own best time? And even though I was back to where I had been before May, I was discouraged that I wasn't able to beat that barrier of my own fastest time three years prior. I still had my 400 IM to go, and it was the last day of the meet. I jumped in, warmed up, and placed first in the prelims. Already, I was annoyed. It was becoming usual for me to get first in prelims only to lose that spot in the finals. In fact, that seemed to be my norm. I didn't want to go into another race seeded first only to hit the wall and have that ranking burst like a balloon the second I looked up at the results. I was done.

That night I started to swim during the warm-up session with Coach Troy. Usually I did a few 50 meters at pace to get my blood flowing and my muscles moving. But I was swimming the slowest times I had ever swum. On my breaststroke I should have been holding a 39-second pace but I was barely making it to the wall at 44 seconds. I was five seconds off in a 50, which meant that if I went that pace during the race, I'd be piling on a whole lot more than 15 extra seconds like I had in May. But it didn't matter. I couldn't make my brain force my body to go faster. "What's wrong with you?" Coach Troy asked.

I didn't want to be there anymore. "I'm just over it."

"What do you mean you're over it?"

"I should have won the 200 backstroke." I saw the way his face folded into a more serious expression. "Or at least gotten second," I added, trying to be more reasonable.

"Get your head in the game, and get into gear," Coach Troy yelled at me. Coach Troy was encouraging, sincere, and always fair. He never lost his temper without just cause, and his voice was raised louder than I had ever heard it before. "You have a chance to swim at World Championships tonight," he said. "The World Championships, tonight," he repeated. "You're going in seeded first and you want to tell me you're over it because what, the 200 backstroke didn't go exactly how you wanted it to go? This is a different day and an entirely different event. Get into gear, and do it now," he said. Then he turned and walked away.

I had no idea how to respond. Coach Troy had never just turned his back and left during a workout session of any kind, especially not during warm-ups at the World Championships. Not knowing what else to do, I got out of the pool. I moped over to the team area, and when I saw Coach Troy approach me, I wondered if he was about to yell at me again. Coach Troy was someone I admired and respected, and I didn't doubt that if he was angry, I deserved whatever was coming. I just couldn't fix the lack of motivation that had taken over. When he opened his mouth, I braced myself.

"Elizabeth, just do one thing tonight."

I would have done anything he said at that point. All I wanted was someone to tell me what to do, because I certainly hadn't the faintest idea how to proceed.

"Just have fun. Just smile, enjoy it. Even if you don't have the greatest race, have fun doing it. That's why you're here. Remember what I told you? You're a racer. So forget about the pace, that doesn't mean anything. Just have fun."

I stood there perplexed. Just have fun? Fun? Fun. Right. I remembered fun. Not going out partying on campus, but those days when I could barely keep from bursting from sheer joy when we pulled up to the pool for practice. That intrinsic feeling of completion being in the water used to give me, before my pace mattered, or my times dictated whether or not my swim was good or bad. Any day in the pool used to be a great day, and I hadn't started swimming to be a champion. That's not what the goal had been at the beginning. The only thing I cared about was being in the water, and before all of the meets, and the qualifiers, and the intervals, and the technical training, and the rankings, and the crowds, the water had been enough. That was all I wanted when I started swimming, and somewhere along the way I had completely lost sight of that simple happiness that had drawn me to the pool in the first place.

The rest of the time before my race, I clung to those three words. Just. Have. Fun. I repeated them over and over and over. I was already at the World Championships, and Coach Troy was right; win or lose, I might as well enjoy the moment. I wasn't swimming great, that was already a given. So, I could pout my way out to the block and sullenly swim alongside athletes who were the best in the world at what they did or I could race. I could do what I loved, soak in every single moment that I was in that pool and hit the wall as fast and as hard as I could, because I was there, and even if I lost, I was still amongst the best of the best.

I had spent enough time throwing up in toilets, worrying myself silly, and imagining every possible thing that could go wrong. Maybe that was what I was over. Walking out to that pool deck, I concentrated on the gleam of the water and vibrant blue of the walls. They were beautiful, and I was standing in front of a crowd that was cheering for me and for all of the other swimmers who had beaten the odds to make it that far. Coach Troy had made his point; this was a moment worth savoring. I did as he said and consciously smiled when I climbed up onto the block and stared down at the pool. Then I dove in and instantaneously nothing else mattered. It was just me, the water, and my strokes. After the 100 fly, I was at the front of the group and I held onto that first place position during the next 100 of backstroke. On breaststroke, which had unquestionably been the most problematic for me, I broke away from all of the other swimmers to carve out a significant lead. And during the last leg of freestyle, I distanced myself farther and farther from my closest competitor. When I finished, I didn't care what happened. I knew I had given that swim everything I had, but the thunderous applause of the crowd was the icing on the cake for what was one of my most phenomenal swims. Coach Troy's words and remembering my love for the sport had put me in a totally different mindset. I swam the fastest time of my life, and that day I became a World Champion.

This is me, living up to my nickname, "The Fuss." I was a ball of energy and loved making a simple meal a complete disaster for my parents.

My beautiful mother, Joanie, and me in our backyard pool. I was about eight months old and obsessed with the water. Time in the pool seemed to cure all of my tantrums as a child.

At the age of three, I became fascinated with music and the violin. Outside of the water, playing the violin was the only other time I would calm down and behave. I still play to this day.

*Coach Josh, my teammate Chiara, and me at the 1999 New
England Swimming Championships in Springfield, MA.
This man changed my world.*

*November 2000. I'm holding my first Olympic medal.
I remember clinging on to it and thinking to myself, "I
will win one of these one day." Talk about confidence.*

In my happy place.

Carl, the man that pushed me to my furthest limits while making sure I still had fun. He is one of the jolliest, most brilliant people I know.

Laura and me at a Bluefish dual meet in high school. She is still one of my best friends to this day and has always been there for me through thick and thin. I absolutely love this girl.

This was the moment I became an Olympian in 2008. I am hugging Katie Hoff, who had just broken the World Record and qualified for her second Olympic Games. This woman was one of my first friends on the National Team and remains one of my closest friends to this day.

Chuck and me on the pool deck at the 2008 Beijing Olympic Games.
Words cannot express how grateful I am for this man (and his funky shoes).

Schmitty and me at our first Olympic Games together.
The 2008 Olympics were the start of a lifelong friendship between us.
She is one of the strongest, funniest, most radiant women I know.

Ryan and me being us. He is the big brother I never had but always needed. I think this guy has made me laugh harder than anyone in the world (aside from Schmitty).

Li Xuanxu, Ye Shiwen, and me doing a lap around the stadium in London after winning our Olympic medals in the 400 Individual Medley. Despite the media surrounding the outcome of the race, this was a moment of pure joy.

Mom, me, Danny, and Dad at the 2012 London Olympic Games after I won my first Olympic medal. It takes a village to make a dream come true, and, through the ups and downs, my family's support never wavered. My medals are just as much theirs as they are mine.

Coach Troy and me having a moment. This man is so much more than just a coach. He is a friend, a mentor, and a father figure. I am incredibly lucky to have him in my life.

Coach Troy and me at our favorite sushi restaurant in Gainesville, FL. We go out to eat often, and the unspoken rule is "I paid last time, so you pay this time." I don't think I've ever paid for a meal because every time he asks with a smirk, "Did you pay last time?" I always laugh and say, "Yes. Yes I did."

Teresa and me in Budapest. She flew all the way to Europe to watch me race in the last swim meet of my career. This woman not only shaped me into a better athlete, but, more importantly, a better human being. Teresa is the big sister and role model I always needed.

The late Mr. Dempsey playing his violin. This man gave me the gift of perspective. He helped me realize life is so much more than swimming, and that music is the universal language that brings us all together. He is an angel in my life.

CHAPTER ELEVEN

Once the 2011 World Championships were over, there was no down time. Typically, after World Championships, we would have a two-week break to relax and reset for the next season, but this year was different. From Shanghai I flew directly to Palo Alto, California. Nationals were being held at Stanford University, and two days after my plane landed I swam the full meet. After Nationals, I flew to the Olympic Training Center in Colorado Springs for a two-week training camp with the University of Florida. This year, everything mattered just a little bit more and the energy felt different. Trials for the 2012 London Olympic Games were 12 months away, and everyone already had qualifying for Team USA on their brain. My teammates and I weren't the only ones looking ahead to London. Coach Troy was adamant that we were starting training for trials early and we were going hard. Coach Troy didn't care how tired we were, he wanted us to work. He had a way of pushing us to our absolute max while remaining encouraging and using positive reinforcement to make us want to do even more so that we could ultimately improve. At times the workouts seemed punishing, but Coach Troy acknowledged the difficulty.

"You're going to work harder than you've ever worked before. Get used to it. You might not like it right now, but it's going to make you better in the long run." When it came to training for the 2012 Olympics, Coach Troy wanted to make sure he put all of us in the best possible position to qualify. Each drill had to be perfect, every turn precise, and the intervals got faster and faster and faster. The dry land training became more challenging, and each one of us was tested over and over and over. He pushed us to our best, and then he pushed us harder. "This is the year that you're going to be amazing."

Once we returned to the University of Florida, fresh from training, I began my sophomore year of college. I took Coach Troy seriously. And he'd probably be surprised to know how often I thought back to my visit and our conversation before I ever joined the team. "Do you want to be an Olympic Champion?" Those words were cemented in my mind. I did. I had never wanted anything so badly, and I was driven by the actuality that I might have a real shot. That year I kept my head down and trained as hard as I could. When I wasn't in the pool, I was studying, and I didn't let my new healthy lifestyle slip. It wasn't always easy. I knew the other students were going out, partying like I had the year before, and having the time of their lives. But I wanted the Olympics so badly that I was blind to almost everything else. The only other place where I focused my attention was on my studies, and even with the training, I remained a straight "A" student. But the balance I used to pride myself on maintaining was something I eventually had to give up. I lived and breathed swimming, and the only reason my grades remained so high was that I scheduled my study time in just like I did practice—it was nonnegotiable. As the months went on, I continued to keep my eye on the prize, qualifying for the 2012 Olympic Games.

That year was a blur. I swam, ate, slept, studied, ate, went to class, swam, ate, slept, and repeated. I was the most disciplined I had ever been, and my entire life had a singular purpose; I wanted to be an Olympic Champion. I could still see the look on Coach Troy's face when he asked me that question and recall the cool confidence he had exuded. From the first time I had watched the Sydney Olympic Games in my living room when I was seven years old, that had been my goal. Josh had told me to be unrealistic in what I wanted to achieve, and I was on the brink of living out my biggest, wildest dream. There wasn't anything that was going to stop me. The previous NCAA season had been my best ever, but my sophomore year made my first season at the University of Florida pale in comparison. It seemed like every day I was getting faster, and I was in better shape than I had ever been before. I won all three of my events at the 2012 Southeastern Conference Meet, and I won the 200 backstroke at the 2012 NCAA Championships. Once again, after the NCAA Championships was over, I was floating on cloud nine, but I had learned from my mistake the previous year.

Winning an NCAA Championship for Florida meant a lot to me, but the last thing I wanted to do was celebrate. I knew better than to jeopardize my chance to make the Olympic team by hitting the party scene. If anything, I was grateful that my shenanigans freshman year had reinforced how important taking care of my body was if I wanted to perform at my peak. That was a lesson that was invaluable when it came to preparing for trials. After the NCAA Championships, I didn't drink a drop of alcohol. I didn't eat one bad meal. I never stayed up late, and I didn't go out. Nothing was more important to me than the Olympics and whenever I was tempted, I replayed Coach Troy's question in my mind, like the scene of a movie I'd seen a thousand times before. It was all I needed to be reminded of what I really wanted—to stand on the podium at the Olympic Games. The faster I swam, the more disciplined I became. Improving my times only made me that much more motivated to keep doing all of the right things. Olympic years, the stakes are higher. In a sport that's only relevant once every four years and where tenths of a second can make or break your opportunity to compete, there's no room for careless errors, mediocre form, or slacking at practice. And I was exactly where I needed to be. Everything was adding up. I was healthy; I only continued to get stronger, and I was consistently putting up phenomenal times. It was becoming more and more clear that I had a realistic shot at winning gold for the USA at the Olympic Games.

In 2012, the Olympic Trials were held in Omaha, Nebraska, at the same venue as they were in 2008. The Qwest Center had been renamed The CenturyLink Center, but the theatrical nature of the event hadn't changed. Thousands of people packed the stands which surrounded the 50-meter pool. Music pulsed throughout the arena, the slim black pieces of metal which shot tongues of fire lined the pool deck, cameras were strategically setup to capture the races, and the lights were dimmed everywhere except for the luminous rectangle of water where the races took place. The name of the venue wasn't the only thing that was different. Four years prior, when I had arrived as an inexperienced 15-year-old hoping to qualify for my first Olympics, felt like a million years ago. When I had come to trials in 2008, the expectations had been minimal. I was expected to qualify in backstroke, but as a newbie that wasn't a given, and I had stunned the swimming world and myself by securing my spot in the 400 IM. In 2008, I had everything to gain and nothing to lose, but that no longer seemed to be the case. The swimming world now knew who I was, and I had heard my name announced over and over again by commentators as "the favorite" for gold when it came to the 400 IM. Four years ago, I didn't think I had a shot at qualifying in that event, now I was going in as the defending World Champion.

I remembered the nervous and uncontrollable surges of adrenaline which had plagued me at the last Olympic Trials there. It was humbling to think about how overwhelming walking into the enormity of trials had been as a 15-year-old. As the crowd roared and the lights flashed throughout the darkly lit stadium, I was proud of how far I had come. I swam prelims that morning, put up a great time, and came in first. But unlike four years ago, the win wasn't a surprise and I was able to keep my nerves in check. That afternoon I ate a Jimmy John's sub for lunch (Beach Club #12 was my favorite), took a nap, and maintained a calm sense of focus. But no matter how much confidence I had in my ability, my training, and my preparedness, it was still the Olympic Trials. One mistake could cost me my shot at even competing for Team USA, and after all of the hard work, training, energy, time, and effort I put in, not making the cut would be devastating. I tried to push those doubts aside as I returned to the pool that night for finals. When I dove in for my first warm-up, everything went well. I felt good in the water; I wasn't running to the bathroom to throw-up, and things seemed to be going as smooth as could be expected.

I made my way back to our team area, and that's when the pressure hit. One minute I was seated and ready to go, the next it was if the entire sky had caved in and fallen down on top of me. As the clock slowly ticked closer to race time a funnel of doubts and uncertainties tornadoed through my mind. What if I didn't make it? What if I made a mistake and blew my chances at qualifying? What if someone just like me four years prior was waiting to surprise the world and smoke my best time? I wanted the Olympics with every single part of my being, and the thought of it being taken away that night was so terrifying that I suddenly felt paralyzed. I couldn't stop the accompanying wave of panic from washing away my sense of composure and I started to cry uncontrollably. My entire body heaved as I tried unsuccessfully to catch my breath and get a grip. One of our assistant coaches at Florida, Coach Wilby, noticed what was happening and came over immediately.

"What's going on, Elizabeth?" he asked, his words coated in a thick British accent.

I could barely speak, but in between sobs I managed to tell him in broken words how nervous I was for the swim that was now less than 30 minutes away.

Taking a seat beside me, Coach Wilby helped me catch my breath. Then he leaned into me closer, as if what he was about to say was of the utmost importance. "You don't think that they're all scared of you?"

The tears stopped. I was so nervous about how I would swim in trials I hadn't taken into account that I had become the person to beat. While I had been obsessing over what could go wrong, it hadn't crossed my mind that my competitors' biggest fear might very well be me.

"You're the defending World Champion. You're no longer the hunter, you've now become the hunted," he explained. "Sure, that comes with more pressure, but you've got to rise to the occasion if you want to be a champion."

You've now become the hunted. Those words echoed in my mind. For so long I had been the scrawny 13-year-old who no one wanted to talk to outside of the pool or the scrappy 15-year-old who had qualified for the team when I wasn't supposed to. In those four years since I had last stood there at the pool in Omaha, Nebraska, I had gone from unlikely qualifier to the gold medal favorite. Coach Wilby was right, that was a lot of pressure, but I had earned that title and I had worked hard to walk into the 400 IM as the number one swimmer in the world. Maybe there was still that sliver of doubt, which had always told me I wasn't good enough or I shouldn't be there. But wrapping your mind around the fact that you're the best in the world at anything is a hard pill to swallow. Sure, it makes you feel, well, on top of the world. But it's a lofty title to carry, and the second you win, your competitors are already lining up to challenge your place and beat your time. Everyone wants to be number one, but the thing is, even once you win a World Championship, you're still human. There wasn't some magical switch that flipped once you hit a certain number of swims or won an exact quota of races. When the stakes were that high, nerves and anxiety were inevitable, at least they were for me. But Coach Wilby was right. I had a title to defend.

I got my head back on straight and went to put on my racing suit. If I was the person to beat, then bring it on. I was the World Champion, and I wasn't going to lose the title without giving that race everything I had. If everyone was scared of me, I was wasting my time being frightened of myself. All I could do was get up on that block and race my heart out. If I lost, I'd do so knowing that I couldn't have worked harder or trained more. And I liked the idea of being the hunted. Before, I had known I had something to lose, but Coach Wilby's words made it sound more like I had something to protect. I would fight down every inch of that pool, and if I saw anyone gaining on me I'd have to revert to my sheer ability as a racer. My pace times meant nothing, just like Coach Troy had said. It didn't matter what it took. I would rise to the occasion. When I got to the warm-up pool to touch the water for a second time, the desire to win quickly overtook my apprehension and hammered away my doubts. I tried to psych myself up and as I jumped in, I noticed the large screen that hung over the pool which broadcast the trials live. I did a few laps, and then watched the television.

The first race of the meet was the men's 400 IM and Ryan Lochte, my pseudo big brother and University of Florida teammate, was swimming. So I was preoccupied with what was happening in real time. I knew Ryan would make the team, but I wanted to see him qualify, and I was elated to see him touch the wall and win the event. Ryan was the first person named to the 2012 USA Olympic Team, and I thought my heart would burst with pride. I swam a few more fifties at pace, and already I could feel the tingling excitement propel me faster through the water. Ryan made the team. He made the team first. Watching him win inspired me, and not only was I incredibly happy for him, he made the feat that I wanted to accomplish a few minutes later seem possible. We trained together, we swam together, and if he could do it, I could too. The next race was the men's 400 free. Again, I got distracted and found myself holding onto the wall and craning my neck to look up at the big screen. Two of my other teammates from the University of Florida, Peter Vanderkaay and Conor Dwyer, were up. I held my breath as I watched them take their mark and dive off the blocks. I had to deliberately stop myself from screaming at the top of my lungs as they swam up and down the pool on the big screen overhead. I couldn't believe it when they came in first and second. Staring up at the television, it was almost impossible to contain my enthusiasm. The first three swimmers named to the 2012 USA Olympic Team were my friends, my teammates, and they were all coached by Gregg Troy. My event was next. I could be the fourth person coached under Gregg Troy to make the Olympic team in one night. There was no way I could let down Coach Troy or my teammates.

As I stood waiting for the booming of the microphone to announce my lane, I kept picturing Ryan, Peter, and Conor as they touched the wall and the huge smiles that had spread across their faces once they finished. It was as if their victories were contagious. They had lit a spark within me that made it difficult to even stand still. All I wanted to do was dive into the water, hit the wall first, and be the fourth Florida Gator to qualify for the 2012 USA Olympic Team. My only objective when I walked out onto that pool deck was to win. I don't remember much of that race, the only thing on my mind was getting first place. And I did, by almost four seconds. When I slammed my hand onto the wall, the crowd erupted in applause and rose to their feet. I was the fourth person to be named to the Olympic Team, and I was also the fourth swimmer from the University of Florida, coached under Gregg Troy, to qualify that night. To say there was magic in the air for Florida that night would be an understatement. As I stared at the crowd, I tried to soak in the sheer joy that came with becoming an Olympian for the second time.

After the race, I went back to Florida's team area where every single one of my teammates was waiting for me. The people who I trained with day in and day out greeted me with deafening cheers loud enough to make everyone in the warm-up pool turn their heads. "Way to go!" "You did it!" "Awesome swim!" "Go Gators!" "Team USA!" Ryan climbed out of the pool, gave me a massive bear hug from behind and picked me up. "Beisel! Beisel! Beisel!" he chanted. Once he put me down, Ryan whispered into my ear. "I knew you'd get first, lil' sis. Now, let's go to London and win!" Turning towards him, I nodded, still glowing from my first place finish. I believed he could win, and for the first time in my career I believed I could too. Then and there I decided that Ryan and I would go to the Olympics and win the 400 IM, together.

I couldn't have wished for a better day. Not only had I qualified first in my event but making the USA Olympic Team with my friends and teammates made my accomplishment that much sweeter. I felt unbelievably fortunate to have Gregg Troy as my coach. There was no doubt that he had made me a better athlete, and the fact that so many of his swimmers had already qualified for the Olympics on day one of trials was a true testament to his coaching abilities and the program he had built. I was so lucky to be part of his team, and now we were all on our way to London. By the time we finally arrived back at our hotel, I was as exhausted as I was overjoyed. And just as I was about to drag my blissfully tired self to my hotel room for bed, Coach Troy caught my attention. "Meet in the team room in five minutes," he said.

I looked up at him and nodded. I was too tired to be overly curious, so I made my way to the hotel suite that was usually used for team meetings or to grab a quick snack. When I got there, it was me, Ryan Lochte, Peter Vanderkaay, and Conor Dwyer, the other three Gators who had just qualified for the team. Those three guys had become my big brothers. I trained with them every single day, and I knew I was in that room because of them. They had upped my game in practice and constantly pushed me to improve. I immediately ran into Conor's arms. This was his first time making the Olympic team, and I couldn't have been more proud of him. "You did it, Conor!" I cried at the top of my lungs. "Welcome to the club!"

Peter and Ryan, who had both qualified for their third Olympic team that night, started nudging Conor. "Dude, where are you gonna get your tattoo? You know you have to get one." In the middle of us giddily trying to decide where Conor should get his Olympic rings tattoo, Coach Troy walked in. He stood in front of us with an expression on his face that was more serious than usual, and an ambiguous silence blanketed the room. "I want each of you to know how proud I am of what you achieved today," he said. "I called you all in here because I have something to tell you."

I held my breath, hoping that our ideal first day at trials wasn't about to be tarnished. I searched Ryan, Peter, and Conor's faces for guidance, and all of them seemed to be held in suspense as well, their eyes focused on Coach Troy.

Then Coach Troy smiled widely. "I've been named the head USA Swim Coach for the Olympic Games this summer in London."

I wasn't aware that it was possible to feel happier than I did when I had walked into that pow wow with Coach Troy. All of us cheered and huddled around him, and my heart was completely full.

"This is what you've worked so hard for, and I know how much London means to you. I promise I'm going to do everything possible to make us the most successful Olympic swim team in history."

Chills shot up and down my spine, and I knew that I was exactly where I should be. It felt as if the stars had aligned—from the first time I made the USA National Team and had worked with Coach Troy to sitting there in the hotel that night. Deep down in my bones, I was certain that I had made the right choice by going with Gregg Troy and choosing to swim for the University of Florida. My entire life, every decision I had ever made, had put me right there in that room with Coach Troy and three of the best swimmers in the world. We had trained together, we would go to the Olympics together, and unlike last time, I was experienced, I was prepared, and everything was falling into place. There was not a doubt in my mind. I was going to win gold in London.

CHAPTER TWELVE

The rest of trials went well and in addition to qualifying for the 400 IM, I got second to Missy Franklin in the 200 backstroke. So, I would be competing in two events at the London 2012 Summer Olympics. Unlike the first time I had made the team, I knew what to expect. So instead of being nervous about what was to come, I was able to relax and savor the experience. Not to mention, I was stoked to be traveling to London with Coach Troy and teammates who felt like family. In addition to Ryan, Conor, and Peter, Schmitty had also made the team, and I was thrilled that we would be rooming together. From trials, we flew to a training camp in Vichy, France for two weeks. This was right around the time when various other sports teams and groups were making their own parody versions of Carly Rae Jepsen's famous "Call Me Maybe" song. Some of my teammates came up with the idea to do one for the USA Olympic Swim Team. Our videographer, who worked with us doing race footage, offered to film us, and we had an absolute blast lip-syncing and figuring out various lines. It was a hilarious distraction and gave us something fun to do during our off time. Everyone got really into it, and we finished filming the video during our flight to London.

When we arrived for the 2012 Summer Olympic Games it was a sunny July afternoon. "Alright," Schmitty said to me when we landed. "This is our year."

I knew she was right. We had promised ourselves we would come back stronger than ever on our plane ride home from Beijing, and that's exactly what we had done. Going into those games, I was exactly where I wanted to be. Grinning at her, I couldn't wait to see what London had in store for us. "Yes! I'm so ready. What do you think the village will be like?"

Schmitty shrugged as we got off the plane. "I guess we'll know soon enough."

After retrieving our luggage, we piled on a bus with the rest of Team USA and headed to the Olympic Village. Once we arrived, the entire city seemed alive with the spirit of the Olympics. The five interlaced rings were displayed everywhere you looked; on buses, billboards, the sides of buildings, even our bedspreads proudly boasted the symbolic design along with the words "London 2012." Our room was a massive suite that had a big screen television, a kitchenette, and a sitting room with two plush couches that we used for lounging and painting our nails in between practice times. We were on the 12th floor and had a bird's eye view of the entire village, which was especially breathtaking during the evenings when the sun slowly sank beneath the horizon line.

Schmitty and I decided to explore after we dumped our suitcases in the room and attempted to stuff the massive amount of Team USA gear we had accumulated into the dressers beside our beds. The village itself was quaint and picturesque, lined with mazes of sidewalks which zigzagged through lush greenery, complete with plenty of tables and chairs where you could relax in the sun. There were outdoor food stands setup throughout the village, giving it a Sunday morning farmers' market feel. They offered fresh fruits, vegetables, coffees, teas, and smoothies, all for free. We meandered our way through at a leisurely place, taking full advantage of all of the freebies and stretching our legs after the plane ride.

Then we made it to the dining hall. It was inside a massive warehouse-type building filled with loads of food stations labeled by cuisine: Mexican, Italian, Chinese, Jamaican, American, Indian, and Peruvian. And those were only a handful of examples. They had a salad bar in the center filled with containers of colorful greens and every type of topping possible was neatly arranged in endless colorful rows. There was even a cafe where you could have made-to-order lattes, hot chocolate, teas, and more. We ran into Team Australia grabbing food and said a quick hello. For me one of the best things about being on the USA National Team for so long was that I had developed friendships with athletes from other countries all over the world. Unlike in Beijing when I had known almost no one, it was comforting to recognize familiar faces throughout the village and have the opportunity to catch up.

That evening, we went to the venue for our first swim in the Olympic pool. We walked onto the deck in a single file line, wearing our matching United States Olympic Team jackets, pants, and shoes. As soon as a few of us went through the doors, everybody on the pool deck stopped what they were doing and turned their attention to us. Team USA had an incredible amount of talent, and with Coach Troy behind us, I felt unstoppable. We were the team to beat, we knew that and so did everyone else. Coach Troy motioned for all of us to huddle around him behind the starting blocks for a quick meeting. He spoke quietly, but loud enough for us to hear if we leaned in closely. "This is where we become the most successful Olympic team in history. You have all swum in a pool exactly like this before. There's nothing to be nervous about. Every single one of you is already the best in the world because you were able to make the USA Olympic Team. Now, get out there and do it for your country." With that, he squeezed his way out of the middle of the huddle, leaving us with the thought that in less than 72 hours, we would be competing for the United States of America at the Olympic Games.

That night our videographer uploaded the USA Swim Team "Call Me Maybe" video to YouTube. I was with all of the girls, hanging out in a common room, and we loved the final product. "Man, I hope we get at least 1000 views," Schmitty said. "Wouldn't that be awesome?"

"I know," another girl replied. "If we don't have over that tomorrow, we should just take it down."

We went to bed that night and by the time we woke up the next morning, our video had over one million views. None of us could believe it. That video was not only a great way for our team to bond, but we were able to capture our experience at camp and show the world what a great time we had as a team preparing for the Olympics.

Unlike in Beijing, everything seemed to be lining up in my favor. I was training incredibly fast. I was comfortable with the structure of the Olympic Games, and I knew how to navigate the technicalities that came with such a massive event. Schmitty and I were hitting it off even better than I had hoped, and I was at "home" practicing with Coach Troy and my teammates from the University of Florida. Going into those Olympic Games, I felt solid. I was putting up extraordinary times, I was in the best shape of my life, and I knew that Teresa was right. I had put my trust in Coach Troy, and he had made me a better swimmer than I had believed was possible. In London, a well-earned confidence that I had never before been capable of mastering took over. This was my year, and even walking down the street or doing laps in the warm-up pool felt as if they were a part of something magnificent.

The events were ordered in the same sequence they had been in 2008, which meant that the 400 IM would be held on the first day of competition. Instead of attending the opening ceremony, Conor, Schmitty, and I stayed in our team room in the Olympic Village and watched it on television with the rest of the world. The opening ceremonies took place in the Track and Field stadium, which was so close to the Olympic Village, I could feel the boom of the fireworks in my chest as they exploded into the air, signifying the official start of the 2012 Olympic Games. Schmitty looked Conor and I in the eye and grabbed our hands. "Let's do this." We both nodded, knowing exactly what our job was that week—to represent the United States of America. Wanting to be fresh for our swims the next day, we went to bed early once the opening ceremony was over. The next morning, I felt nothing like I had four years ago in Beijing. Instead of being shakily nervous and barely able to eat, I was calm, steady, focused. I ate breakfast, showed up at the pool for warm-ups, and dove in with the confidence that I had always wished I could muster before a huge scale event like the Olympics. There was something that had shifted. I knew that I was the best. I could put up times better than anyone else swimming the event, and I had trained for the last 12 months to develop a relentless stamina which allowed for endurance that I could barely believe myself. There had been so many instances before when I had questioned my readiness, my talent, my training, or my mentality—but not that day. I had never felt more poised and optimistic going into a race, and I was ready.

Sitting in the ready room preparing for my prelim race, I watched the television in the corner that broadcast the races live. I stared at the swimmers who were about to go and watched the heat before me swim the women's 400 IM. There was a swimmer whom I had never heard of named Ye Shiwen from China who caught my eye. She was fast, there was no doubt about it, and when she finished, I glanced at her time. She had swum a 4:31 (four minutes and 31 seconds), which is a remarkable time. Under any other set of circumstances, that might have been enough to get under my skin and flare up my prerace jitters. But not that day. I was the best, and I wasn't going to let anything shake the belief I had in my ability to win. Looking at the small screen, I shrugged. Alright. You want to play? Let's go. I walked out to the pool when my lane was announced, climbed up onto the block and went a 4:31 as well, out touching her time by a few tenths of a second. That put me in the top spot for finals and I couldn't have felt better about my swim. My strokes were long and easy, and I was strong in the water. I couldn't wait to do it again that night at finals.

For the first time before any big meet I was able to sleep through the entire afternoon, which would give me the recovery I needed to go my fastest. I was surprisingly calm, but I was on my game. I had done absolutely everything within my power to put myself in the most advantageous position possible going into that race. I knew that night was my chance. I had wanted to be an Olympic

Champion for as long as I could remember, and I wasn't going to miss my opportunity to win gold for the United States of America. This was my time. This was my race. Listening to music on the way to the venue, I replayed everything that had led up to that moment. I thought back to the 7-year-old version of myself, sitting in front of the television, staring in awe at the Sydney Olympic Games. Deep down, I knew I had surpassed the odds in order to make the dream of becoming an Olympian a reality, and there was a reverent sense of gratitude that came with knowing I had achieved that goal.

I knew it wasn't just me, or one qualifying race. It was 100 million different things that had all added up together. It was Josh's thorough instruction from the very beginning, and his laid back encouragement that made me believe the Olympics could be a possibility. It was every time my parents made that 45-minute drive one way or shuttled me to meets when they could have been doing anything else. It was Carl pushing me and getting my strokes that much stronger, and Chuck making me swim with the seniors even when I preferred to stay with the swimmers my own age. It was Nelson waving his gold medal in front of my face, telling me to believe in myself, and Laura helping me into my racing suit and talking me down before the biggest race of my life. It was every lap, every practice, every drill, and every pointer for every stroke and turn that I had received over the years. It was Teresa encouraging me and helping me climb out of my rut, and when Schmitty and I had promised ourselves we would return with a vengeance after we left Beijing in 2008. It was every time I had chosen swim over everything else. And it was Coach Troy pushing me beyond what I thought I was capable of and molding me into the swimmer I had become. Thinking about all the people who had been there along the way and the various events which had led up to that moment made me profoundly grateful.

Walking into the Aquatics Center, I was determined to win. After we checked in and made our way to the pool, my assurance remained. And before I jumped in for warm-ups, Coach Troy pulled me aside. "Elizabeth, you've got this. Just stay focused, and do what we've practiced. If you touch first at the 300 after breaststroke, you're winning a gold medal tonight." I looked up at him and smiled. We both knew I could do it, and it was easy to see my nerves were under control and I was confident. With that he gave me a massive hug and I swam my warm-up just like any other meet.

Sitting in the ready room, I thought about what Coach Troy had said. He was arguably the greatest coach in the world, and I was certain of what he said. If I could just touch first at the 300, the gold medal was mine. It had been a long road, but I had done the work and was finally ready to rise to the occasion when it came to my racing anxiety. Sitting there, minutes away from my event, I knew that my wildest dream was about to come true. The venue was jam-packed with people, and everyone was enthusiastically cheering and screaming, waving various colored flags and poster board signs. My entire family was in the stands. My brother Danny was sitting with the Olympic snowboarder, Shaun White, and even Bill Gates was watching. Once they announced my lane, I walked out and waved to the crowd. I was ready to dive in and show everyone that I could rise to the occasion, and make it known that not only was I the best, but I could handle that type of pressure. I went into that race the World Champion but I was going to leave the Olympic gold medalist.

I stretched my arms out one final time before climbing onto the block. "Take your mark." Lunging forward, I positioned myself for my dive. "Beep." We were off. The first 100 of butterfly I paced myself and stayed towards the back, but the pack remained fairly even. Going into backstroke was where I would make my move. I made the transition and pulled ferociously, my arms cutting cleanly through the water, each stroke bringing me closer to the lead. By the end of backstroke, I had surpassed every swimmer except for Katinka Hosszu from Hungary who was in the lane next to me. I hit the wall, pushed off and during the first 50 of breaststroke I took the lead. When I realized I had secured the top spot, I revved up my pace and pushed myself as hard as I could. I made each pull concise and glided easily through the water, moving away from the rest of the competitors. By the time I touched the wall at the 300, I had a substantial lead. I was first, and I was sure that I was first by a lot. My heart skipped a beat when I completed that turn, knowing that I was about to be an Olympic gold medalist.

Once I hit the freestyle leg, a second wind came with knowing that I was about to do what I had dreamed about since I was a little girl. One hundred meters left and I had accomplished the goal I had spent the last twelve years chasing. Despite that I knew I was first, I willed myself to go faster. I wanted to go as fast as possible, and I was literally thrashing through the pool doing everything possible to hold onto as much water as I could. Just a little farther and I was there. This was it. Olympic Gold. Finally. But halfway into the first 50 of freestyle, I saw a splash next to me out of the corner of my eye. It wasn't possible. No one was supposed to be able to catch me if I could hold onto the lead until the 300. And I had. I snuck a quick peek and there she was. It was Ye Shiwen from China in the lane next to me. She was gaining on me, and I started to panic. Was I slowing down? Am I dying? How could she have caught me after the 300? All I could do was fight. I kicked harder, I tried to lengthen out my strokes and get more distance from each movement. It didn't feel like I was slowing down, in fact, I felt fast and strong. But even so, she caught me. For a few seconds I held on and we swam side by side, battling it out for the first place spot. But by the time we touched the wall after the first 50 of freestyle, she had overtaken me. Not only had she passed me, but she had done so with so much momentum that I felt as if I had literally stopped moving. I tried with everything I had to catch her, but she only kept pulling farther and farther away.

When we hit the wall, I stared blankly up at the scoreboard. What just happened? Ye Shiwen had broken the world record in the women's 400 IM, and I had come in second. Second? But I touched first at the 300. Did the training not work? Had I choked on my freestyle? Was I not as strong as I thought? What went wrong? Ye Shiwen was smashing the water with excitement, but I was so shocked that I couldn't take my eyes off of the results. I had just won my first Olympic medal, but I couldn't help but feel disappointed. The only thing I wanted to know was my time on the last 100 freestyle. It should have been an insanely proud moment for me, but I was completely blindsided and totally miffed as to how I had failed to come in first. The magic and certainty I had felt since arriving in London exploded into a thousand pieces and twisted and turned sharply in my stomach. I had wanted to be the best, I was there, and I had been the best, but then in a blink of an eye I wasn't. Swallowing my disbelief, I plastered on a smile. I hugged my competitors and since I couldn't speak Ye Shiwen's language, I gave her a congratulatory thumbs up.

On the pool deck, I tried to shake everything off before I went to the mixed zone where I'd have to talk to the media before returning to my team. I forced myself to take deep breaths. I left everything I had in that pool, that much I knew. I swam the best race I could, and sometimes that just had to be enough. After all, I reasoned with myself, I did win an Olympic medal. Trying to be a good sport, I braced myself for the media. Immediately I had cameras and microphones in my face. Not a single interviewer congratulated me on my silver medal. "What happened in the last 100?" "Did you see her coming?" "You were the favorite for gold, how does it feel to win silver instead?" The questions kept firing at me, and I tried to hold it together and answer them as quickly and politely as I could. I hadn't even had five minutes to process the race and all I wanted to do was find Coach Troy. Then a particularly loud man asked me a question I hadn't expected. "Do you think she's doping?" Once he spoke those words, the rest of the media quieted. When I didn't answer, he repeated himself. "Ye Shiwen, do you think she's doping?"

CHAPTER THIRTEEN

I had no idea how to respond to the reporter who asked me if I thought Ye Shiwen was doping. Unfortunately, using illegal substances to boost performance is becoming an all too relevant topic in contemporary sports. But I had never had the issue pressed so directly in my face. I had been part of the international competitive circle of swimming for years, and I hadn't even heard of Ye Shiwen before trials. I didn't know her at all. I certainly was not privy to what she had or had not done when it came to anything. Standing in the middle of a huge cluster of media who eagerly awaited my answer, I did what I had been trained to do since joining the National Team at 13. I masked my raw emotion and didn't let the pain of losing or the shock which was still reverberating show. "It was a great race, and it was just such an honor being able to represent the United States."

What I said was the truth. Swimming for the USA was the most amazing and humbling honor I could imagine. And I was crushed that I wasn't able to do what had been expected of me—win gold. In the moment, I brushed the doping comment aside, still trying to make sense of what had just occurred. I left the mixed zone with my thoughts and emotions in total disarray. I had no idea how to feel about anything. When I made it back to the team area, Coach Troy was waiting. Without a word he took both of my cheeks in his hands and then enveloped me in a huge hug. Still reeling from the race, I couldn't even return the embrace. I just stood there limply, until he let go. Finally, I looked up at him. "What was my last 100 freestyle split?"

"1:01.0," he answered. I was floored. I thought I had messed up, choked on my last 100, and let everyone down. But that was the fastest 100 freestyle split I had ever swam. It made no sense. If I was that fast, how fast was she?

"What was her split?"

"58.6."

My jaw dropped. That wasn't just a fast time. It was the fastest split I had ever heard of anyone achieving.

"She out split every single man who swam tonight; Phelps, Lochte, all of them."

"But how?"

Coach Troy placed his hand on my shoulder. "All that matters is that you swam the greatest race of your life tonight. You were never going to beat a 58.6 split. There wasn't even a chance, so don't beat yourself up. You train with Ryan every single day, and you weren't about to out split him no matter how much work you put in. I would never ask you to do a 58.6 split on the last 100 freestyle of a 400 IM. You left it all out there, and I'm so proud of you. You swam your best, and that's all I asked of you. That's all your country asked of you. So for once, just be proud of yourself, Elizabeth."

Hearing Coach Troy's words, I nearly collapsed in relief. I had done my best. He knew it and I knew it, and I hoped that America knew it too. I had put up the absolute fastest time I was capable of, and that day, it wasn't enough to win gold. But the fact that Coach Troy was proud of me made me happy, and knowing that I had swum the greatest swim of my life when it had mattered most made me okay with second place. In a way, I had to be, because I had put so much time, effort, and work into preparing for those four and a half minutes on that world stage. It wasn't gold, but there was a silver lining. I had earned an Olympic medal, and I had put my country's flag on the podium the first night of the Olympic Games, which meant a lot. It was not how I had hoped the 400 IM would go, but I was proud of myself as I stood in between Ye Shiwen and her teammate, Li Xuanxu, who had gotten bronze. I gratefully accepted my medal, waved to the crowd, and soaked in my accomplishment.

That second place had taken a lot of work, and standing there that night I had no regrets.

After the 400 IM I refocused. Although I wished it had been gold, I had medaled and the sparkle of the London Olympics remained despite my second place finish. Schmitty and I were having a blast rooming together, and I attended all of the races to cheer on Team USA. As far as swimming went, the United States was having an amazing Olympics and Schmitty was on fire. She won a total of five medals, including the gold in the 200 free, when she set a new Olympic record. Watching her and the rest of Team USA put up outstanding performances and unbelievable times only made me that much more excited for the 200 backstroke. I was swimming fast in practice, my teammates from the University of Florida were doing great, my backstroke felt on, and Coach Troy was there. Things were going well, but this time my swim had to be on my own terms. After the 400 IM all I wanted from the 200 backstroke was to swim my best time. I couldn't control the competition or determine the outcome of the race. If I got a medal that was great, but for me the 200 backstroke was all about personal improvement.

When I showed up for prelims, I was relaxed and focused. I easily qualified for the semifinals and during semis I went a best time and got seeded first for finals. That best time was all I needed to know that I had succeeded. I was thrilled that I had hit my own personal best and it felt great to have qualified number one for anything at the Olympics. Thinking about that night, I couldn't wait to swim. The pressure was off. I had already won a medal and beat my own best time. I didn't have the usual nervous stomach or raincloud of doubts which hovered over me. I felt like I had before all of the pressure and the expectations had been laid out and anchored me down. There was a childlike excitement that washed over me before finals. The only thing I wanted to do was what I loved most—race. I didn't care about winning at that point. I just wanted to do my best. Whatever happened beyond that, I was willing to accept.

Schmitty found me before my event. "Beisel!"

"Hey!"

"Are you nervous for tonight?" she asked.

"Not really. What about you?" Schmitty had a final that night as well.

"I'm feeling good. But you know what we should do?"

Shaking my head, I had no idea. Schmitty and I were always messing around, so I was curious what she had in mind. "What?"

"We should drink coffee before our races. Everybody else drinks coffee before their races. Why don't we?"

I grabbed her arm. "Yes! Let's do it." London had an enchanting vibe that made saying yes to something new seem necessary.

Giggling we both purchased a cup of coffee from a nearby vendor. "Cheers," we said, clicking our Styrofoam cups together.

Neither of us had ever had coffee before. Not only were we both naturally incredibly energetic, but we were already practically bouncing off the walls in anticipation for our races that evening. After I had that cup of coffee, I was buzzing with caffeine. Schmitty and I both wished each other good luck then I headed to warm-up for the 200 backstroke. I felt incredible in the water, was still high from my giant cup of dark roast, and I was swimming the fastest pace I ever had. When I arrived in the ready room, I was the least nervous I had been before a race. I sat next to Missy Franklin, a hilarious, tall, blonde swimming powerhouse, who I had become good friends with over the course of our time with Team USA in London. We chatted quietly before our lanes were announced, but when they came to usher us to the pool, she placed her hand on mine and her face grew serious. "We're both getting on that podium tonight," she said.

Maybe it was the coffee, the magnitude of the Olympic Games, the number of hours I had logged in the pool, or just naive optimism—but I found myself nodding. Why not? I wasn't sure where my nerves had gone, or when I had transformed from throwing up in the bathroom to craving the spotlight that came with walking out in front of the crowd. But there was nothing holding me back or dragging me down. It was the opposite. The water was where I thrived and this was just another chance to show that to the world and myself. Missy and I walked out when they called our names, waved to the stands filled with thousands of cheering fans, and took our places behind our respective blocks. We both had an incredible swim. Missy broke the world record and won gold, and I surprised myself by coming in third and winning my second Olympic medal. I even beat the best time I had swum the night before. I was on cloud nine and beyond elated that not only was I going to receive a bronze medal, but also that Missy had won gold.

The Awards Ceremony that night remains one of the most extraordinary experiences of my life. It was the first swim of the Olympics where two Americans had both medaled in the same race, and because of that, there were two American flags on the podium. After accepting our medals, Missy and I both stood in allegiance as our flags were raised and the American anthem played throughout the arena. As I mouthed the words to the song I knew so well, my eyes fell on the pool which glimmered under the fluorescent lights displaying the reflection of two American flags from above. I had never been more proud of my teammate, my country, or myself, and that is a moment Missy and I will share forever. When I won the silver in the 400 IM, I had listened to the Chinese national anthem. This was different. Being able to stand with Missy on that podium, listening to the Star Spangled Banner, and seeing the red, white, and blue flags painted across the water made that Olympic Games for me.

Leaving London was hard. It was only a matter of weeks that I had been gone, but it felt as if I had surpassed an enormous milestone. As I said goodbye to my teammates, I knew that what we had shared together would remain, but I wasn't sure that I wanted it to be over. I was tremendously proud of what I had accomplished, but I was overwhelmed by the sentimentality that accompanied those games.

I was going home with two Olympic medals, and while the gold had eluded me, I knew that I had left my very best in the pool at the Aquatics Center in Queen Elizabeth Olympic Park. Watching as the Olympic Village grew smaller and smaller as we drove away, I knew that the 2012 Summer Olympic Games would always be a part of who I am. It made me an Olympic medalist, it cemented so many new friendships and reaffirmed those I already had, and it was the meet where I finally learned to race for myself and not for the accolades. My best was my best, regardless of where that put me in the competition, and there was peace of mind that came with this newfound knowledge.

Sitting on the plane back home to Providence, everything felt surreal. When I had left for the Olympics, all I wanted was a gold medal, but it felt like I was coming back with so much more. My mind whirled through the blur of days that were now behind me, and I looked forward to arriving home and climbing into my bed. By the time I reached the airport, I was exhausted from traveling, emotionally spent, and a little hungover from celebrating my last night in London. Dragging my luggage behind me, I was surprised to see two police officers dressed in full gear awaiting the plane. They came directly to me. "Elizabeth?"

My stomach did a back flip. Had I done something wrong? "Yes?" I stammered.

We're here to escort you."

"Okay?" I wasn't sure what was happening, but I followed their lead and they took me down a hallway and then opened the door to a large room that was decorated beautifully. It was stocked with champagne, charcuterie boards with a selection of cheeses, endless platters of fruit, and at least a dozen bouquets of flowers, along with a group of people who clapped as soon as I entered. "Congratulations!"

I was completely surprised and a little relieved that I wasn't getting arrested after being pulled aside by the police. "Thank you!" I beamed. It was such a nice gesture and sipping champagne and munching on cheese cubes and chocolate covered strawberries seemed like a good enough reason to postpone my much needed nap.

Finally, the police officers found me again. "Alright, Elizabeth, follow us, right this way."

I shot them a questioning glance, but they gave nothing away, so I followed behind them towards the airport exit. When I walked out of the automatic glass doors, there was a massive 18-passenger limo waiting for me. Both of the police officers gestured for me to get in. One of them opened the door and when I glanced inside, I saw my entire family with huge smiles and more bottles of champagne. "Surprise!"

I immediately jumped in. "You guys!" I hugged and kissed every single one of them, thankful that they had come to the airport to meet me and shocked by the size of the limo they had arrived in. "I can't believe you did this. It feels so good to be home," I said, ready to say hello to my dog and go to bed. "I can't wait to see Chico!"

"Well you're going to have to wait a little bit longer," my dad said, laughing.

"What do you mean?" I asked.

"The whole state is basically waiting for you at North Kingstown High," Danny replied.

"Why?"

My family laughed. "Everyone wants to congratulate you. All of Rhode Island was cheering for you during the Olympics, and they want to meet you. There are literally thousands of people at the high school just waiting for you to arrive. Channel 10 has put together a special welcome home event. It's going to be fun."

Channel 10 was the local news station, and it had not even occurred to me that people would want to see me. I had been so wrapped up in London and the games I hadn't had time to think about what was going on at home. Apparently, thousands of people had gathered at the Willows and countless other places across the state to watch the finals live and support me. I stared down at the sweats I was wearing which were less than fresh after my overnight flight. "I can't go like this! Look at how I'm dressed." I tried to find a mirror. "I'm not even wearing any make-up!"

My mom smiled knowingly and pulled out a duffel bag. "I brought you some clothes and your cosmetics bag."

I made a quick awkward change in the car, and soon I was sipping on champagne in the back of the limo with both of my medals around my neck. Laughing, everything felt light, airy, and fun. I was completely content to be surrounded by the people I loved. I was still tired, but I was flattered that Channel 10 had cared enough to put something together.

I don't know what I was expecting, but when we arrived at North Kingstown High School, I was blown away. The entire football stadium was filled to capacity with people from all over Rhode Island. Loudspeakers that blasted upbeat music lined the field, cameras were aimed in all directions, Channel 10 and every other local news station had their vans parked and reporters ready, and as I walked onto the football field, I was overcome with emotion. Seeing how many people had shown up to welcome me home made every single sacrifice worth it. In a world where so many bad things happen, I had done something that brought people together and gave them a reason to applaud. I shook as many hands as possible and tried to memorize each and every face I saw. Coming from a small state that had few Olympians had given me the enormous gift of unwavering and unparalleled support from people I had never even met. What I did mattered to them, and it would be impossible to put into words how much their encouragement and loyalty has meant to me throughout my career. As I made my way through the crowd, I teared up. The Olympics had made me proud to be an American, but that day, I felt like the luckiest person in the world. What Rhode Island lacked in size, it made up for in heart a million times over.

CHAPTER FOURTEEN

If I thought the attention I received after the Beijing Olympic Games was crazy, coming home from London rocked my world. I stayed in Rhode Island with my parents for about 10 days in August before returning to the University of Florida, and I wasn't able to go anywhere without being recognized. It was impossible to grab a coffee, go to the grocery store, or even get gas without someone stopping me and asking me for a picture or an autograph. Every time I went out to lunch or dinner, various people offered to pay for my meal, and when my family and I tried to eat out there would be a throng of strangers standing around our table who wanted to meet me. I was much younger after Beijing, and I hadn't medaled. Now that I was more grown-up and an Olympic medalist, people seemed more eager to approach me in public. I came home to stacks and stacks of fan mail from all over the world, and relatives I didn't even know I had started contacting me. People wanted my autograph, asked for signed pictures of me, and I had no idea how anyone had even gotten my address. "Whoa! You're a celebrity," Danny said in disbelief. "This is wild!" Danny and my good friends joked that they were my camera crew because whenever we went out they inevitably were the ones tasked with taking photographs when people asked for a picture.

Danny was beyond excited for me and super proud, but my parents never made a huge to-do about the Olympics or my medals. That definitely kept me grounded and didn't let everything go to my head. That week, if we went out to dinner, they acted as if the fanfare was no big deal. "Hey, if it gets too much, we'll just leave." The limelight felt surreal and was a bit disorienting. I had always been a fast swimmer, and I had gone to the Olympics before. Sure, I had won two medals this time but I hadn't changed at all and I hadn't expected things to be so different. Coming back to Rhode Island was like returning to another world. It was awesome because I got to see the billboard wishing me good luck, all of the signs which still stood in people's yards cheering me on, and it was humbling to see firsthand how widespread my support was. However, after those 10 days I was ready to return to the University of Florida and get back to normal.

I had always received more attention from people in my home state than most Olympians, and Rhode Island generously and enthusiastically backed me as one of their only representatives at the Games. At the University of Florida, I was sure I would fade into the backdrop of the enormous campus and be able to refocus on training and school. By the time I had become a Gator, the buzz around the 2008 Olympics had long since died down. So I had never even been asked about Beijing during my time at Gainesville. I was a good swimmer at the University of Florida, but that was not relevant to anyone outside of the team. However, that was all about to change. When I returned to campus, I couldn't even walk to class without people stopping me. "Hey! Are you Elizabeth Beisel?" "Can I get an autograph?" "Great job!" "Mind if I get a picture?" At first, I was taken aback. I had assumed the public recognition would end with leaving Rhode Island, but I was wrong. During the first week of school, I would be sitting in a 300-person lecture hall and the instructor would mention me. "Just to let you know, we do have Olympic medalist, Elizabeth Beisel, in our class. You probably watched her on television over the summer." Everyone would turn, stare at me and clap, as I smiled awkwardly, uncertain of how to respond. In a way, all of the attention was flattering and pretty cool, but it was also never-ending. There was nowhere I could go where people weren't taking pictures of me, pointing me out, asking for autographs, or wanting to hear about London. I was approached walking to class, eating at the dining halls, studying at the library, going out to the bar, and I felt like I could never let my guard down for even a second. No matter what I did or where I went, people were constantly approaching me or even just blatantly staring, and at times, it was draining.

One day after practice when I was feeling particular overwhelmed, Ryan sat down with me. He was used to being noticed regularly when we were walking around campus, out at night, and when we were traveling people were constantly coming up to him at restaurants, in the airport, and pretty much everywhere else. I hadn't noticed it much before, but now I couldn't help but wonder how he always remained so calm and collected. And he had experienced this phenomenon to a much greater degree than I had. "Sometimes, I just want to do my own thing," I said. "Without everyone staring at me or coming up to me everywhere I go."

Ryan sighed. "Do you want some advice?"

I nodded, grateful for any insight on how to handle this new level of attention.

"Look, when I was a little kid, I ran into this swimmer who I absolutely idolized in a hotel elevator. I couldn't believe it. I was so excited and getting an autograph from him would have meant the world to me. But the guy said no. He wouldn't even give me the time of day. I've never forgotten the way that made me feel. It was one of the saddest most disappointing memories of my childhood. So, my suggestion to you is to sign every single autograph that you can. Make someone's day."

What Ryan said resonated with me completely. No matter how tight our schedule was, how many people asked, or what was going on with him, Ryan was always willing to sign an autograph or take a picture. He made time for the people who sought him out and he never ever said no. Now I understood why. Being generous with my time was something I learned from him.

He shrugged. "You never know what someone's going through or how much they may have been cheering you on. A few minutes of your time might mean a lot more than you realize."

After sitting down with Ryan, I decided that I would do the same. My focus had been on how the attention was affecting me, but I hadn't thought about the idea that a moment of my time might really matter to someone else. From then on, every time anyone asked, not only did I say yes, I did so gladly. His words stuck with me. If I could make someone else's day, I would. And the shift that conversation created helped me tremendously. I no longer minded the other students coming up to me on campus and posed with classmates when we were out at the bar. But just as I had begun to get used to the spotlight and the constant recognition, it died down.

That's the thing about the Olympics. You train for years and then for a couple of weeks, the entire world knows your name, your whole country is rooting for you, the media wants interviews, the fan mail comes, and for a while, everyone loves you. But a few months later, once the competition is over, that all goes away. Yes, getting recognized everywhere I went was crazy, but when it stopped, it almost felt like I had done something wrong. After I got back from London everyone was so proud and excited and couldn't get enough of me, and I had definitely been riding on cloud nine. But one day I woke up, and reality hit. People stopped coming up to me and there were no reporters or news stations that wanted to talk to me like there had been in the mixed zone at the games. The teachers who had applauded me now expected me to do well on exams, and I was back to competing for my college team. All the brightness of the limelight dimmed, and it was difficult for me to get back into the groove once that happened. I had been riding high after the Olympics, but that was followed by an exponential low.

I loved the atmosphere of the Olympic Games. Competing on the world stage was where I shined, and the teammates who had become my closest friends were now scattered all over the country. The bonds you form with other athletes when you go through something like the Olympic Games are unique because no matter how hard you try to explain to your family or friends, it's almost impossible to describe the pressures, joy, and even heartbreak that the Olympics bring. I missed everything about the Olympics; getting to room with Schmitty, walking into a crowded arena that roared with applause, the sense of unity Team USA embodied when it came to representing our country, and the dizzying energy the intensity of the competition created. I still was in touch with many of my teammates, but eventually catching up with them happened less and less. A few times, I thought about visiting Schmitty and some of the other girls, but I couldn't miss school or swim practice. And eventually, once we all returned to our normal lives, it was almost as if London had never happened. The Olympics was like a small bubble of existence in which Team USA ruled while the rest of the world watched, but once I was back in the States that bubble burst and I had no way of going back.

Every day that I showed up to practice was a struggle. I didn't talk to anyone on the University of Florida team about what I was going through, but everyone could tell that something was off. I stopped laughing and joking around at the pool, it was all I could do to just get through the workout. My times got slower and when it came to racing, I wasn't going anywhere near where my pace had been previously. Usually swimming was what I looked forward to, but now that it was just another thing on my to-do list. I searched for other ways to get involved that I would enjoy. I had always done well in my coursework, so I sought out opportunities with the journalism school at Florida and started interning at the WUFT News Station for one of my classes. Every Wednesday, it was my job to deliver the local news to Gainesville. I covered stories about politicians, town events, and even sports, and I actually really enjoyed the challenge. Just like with swimming, I liked the idea of being in front of people and I knew I had a knack for performing. There were days when I thought seriously about pursuing a career in broadcast journalism after college. But as exciting and awesome as the prospect of eventually having a real life outside of swimming was, it also terrified me.

I started meeting with Coach Troy once a week. "I don't know what to do. I just can't get excited about swimming." Going from sold-outs arenas with screaming fans back to collegiate swimming was a drag. And I still desperately missed the magic of the Olympics and the magnitude of that caliber of competition.

"Alright," Coach Troy said. "You don't have to fully commit to swimming hard again until December. I'll give you until then to get your head on straight and figure things out. Take care of your mental health first. But once December hits you need to get back into gear because the team needs you."

"Okay." I hoped by that time I could shake my funk and get back into swimming for real. I was on a full scholarship, and my education depended on my swimming because my family couldn't afford it otherwise. And I owed it to the other 26 members of my team to work my way back to my best. With two years still left at the University of Florida, all I could do was go through the motions and hope that my motivation returned. Coach Troy had told me to do the things outside of swimming that brought me joy, and I found myself going back to the violin whenever I had down time. I never really dealt with the post-Olympic lull. I didn't know how. I just tried to block it out, and move on. Those next few months, I would go to the music center, sign up for a room, and play the violin for hours at a time. I liked that no one knew where I was or what I was doing when I was there. And I let myself get lost in the tempo of the music. The violin was therapeutic for me, and those visits to the music center got me through those next few months.

Despite that Coach Troy had told me I needed to get serious about swimming again in December, nothing seemed to click into place for me mentally. Going to practice still seemed more like a job than something I loved and as much as I wanted my heart to be back in the pool, my head wouldn't allow it. That March we had NCAA Championships in Indianapolis, Indiana, at the Indiana University

Natatorium. I wanted to show up for Coach Troy, my teammates, and myself. But as I made my way to the pool deck for my swim, I couldn't work up the exhilaration that used to take over before I raced. I would have given anything to recapture the enthusiasm I had before the 2012 Olympic Games, but I felt like a robot operating on autopilot. Standing on the block before my 400 IM, I stared down at the water. I couldn't help but wonder if my love for swimming had ended with my time in London.

As the months continued and I wasn't able to recapture the usual release swim brought, I found myself reverting more and more to violin. When I wasn't at practice or studying, I went back through all of the pieces of music I used to work on with Mr. Dempsey. I would pick out my favorites, head to the music center, and disappear into the tempo and melodies that had brought me happiness before, when my swimming future was uncertain after Josh had left and I had no idea what came next. When I was concentrating on the notes, I didn't have to think about swimming or how to fix my lack of drive when it came to the water. I forgot about the fact that I hit the wall second when I was supposed to come in first. Nothing else mattered but that moment and whatever music I had in front of me. With the violin, I didn't have to go a certain time, breathe a specific way, or keep my arms at a particular angle. I didn't have to worry about the clock or the interval or the next set. All I had to do was play. Of course, I loved to race. But the nice thing about the violin was that I didn't ever have to lose. I never walked away disappointed or with unfulfilled expectations. At that point, I had swimming and I had school, and music was the only part of my life where the outcome didn't matter and I was able to just let go.

Even when I melted into the music, I could still hear Mr. Dempsey's voice in my head, telling me not to rush and to keep an even tempo. Although I had hated when he used to force me to use a metronome, I was now able to keep a slow and steady pace naturally. I loved spending time in the music center. The few periods in my life when swimming failed to keep me balanced, the violin always got me through. Staring at the pages and pages of music in my room one night, I couldn't help but smile as I thought back to that summer so many years ago when I had spent the entire month of August playing the violin alongside Mr. Dempsey. I recalled the afternoons I spent perfecting my technique, playing concertos and sonatas, and progressing onto more complicated pieces. Those days reminded me of the nights when I would fall asleep listening to Back Partitia or a Haydn concerto on my MP3 player and dream about playing Carnegie Hall in New York City.

That summer, I hadn't had the slightest idea what my future held. Now, even as a two-time Olympian I seemed equally as clueless. But I was thankful to have the violin as an outlet. Music was what helped me through my very darkest times when swimming couldn't. That was a gift that Mr. Dempsey gave me. I still wish I would have made it a point to tell him how much I leaned on music when nothing else made sense and say thank you. Mr. Dempsey passed away before I had the chance to express that to him in words, but I hope deep down he knew. He had a unique appreciation for music, and I think the reason he was such a good teacher was that he loved it so much. To this day, every time I pick up a violin, I think of him and how he used to affectionately call me Vivace. I haven't made it to Vienna yet to play, but one day I will and I know when I do, he'll be watching.

CHAPTER FIFTEEN

After NCAA Championships, I still hadn't recovered from the low that came from losing my Olympic high. I had hoped that eventually things would naturally balance back out, but that didn't seem to be happening. I went to Coach Troy again, afraid that swimming would never hold the allure it had before. I wanted to walk into practice excited, not dragging my feet, just waiting for it to be over.

"It's been months since the Olympics. And nothing's working, I don't feel any better," I said frustrated. "Swimming just isn't the same."

"I don't know what to tell you, Elizabeth. Just keep doing things you love outside of the water and take care of your mental health. If you need a break, take a break."

At that point, I had no idea what I needed. So, I kept coming to practice, doing the drills, hitting the intervals, and trying to remember what had made me love to swim in the first place. I also continued to play the violin as often as possible. But no matter what I did, nothing changed. My mood never got worse, but it wasn't improving either. I was stuck in a sea of indifference, just trying to stay afloat. Finally, Coach Troy came up to me after practice. "Alright. You know what? You're not coming to practice for a few days. I'm giving you the entire weekend off, and you don't have a choice. Don't even think about swimming. I want you to get out of town. Don't go near a pool, don't put on a swim cap, nothing. Just enjoy yourself. Take a mental break. But come back ready to train."

A weekend with no training? I was elated. Not only could I not wait to get away and relax, my coach was telling me to go. That was exactly what I needed. I made plans with five of my girlfriends from the team, and we all decided to go to St. Petersburg, Florida, for the weekend. One of my friends had a house there, and we were going to spend time lounging on the sand, dolphin watching, sunbathing, and hanging out on her boat. There wasn't going to be any talk about swimming or races or times or meets. I was going to be able to do things I never got to do, and I breathed in an enormous sigh of relief at the thought of a mini-vacation. I could let off some steam, catch up with my friends, reset, and be fresh to swim when I got back to Gainesville. It was the perfect remedy to my post-Olympic slump.

As we drove to St. Petersburg that Friday evening, I rolled down the window and the warm wind blew against my cheeks. I hadn't felt that free in a long time, and I was psyched for a weekend off. We chatted the whole drive about what we would do and how nice it would be to just chill. When we woke up on Saturday morning, we had a leisurely breakfast and hung out on the patio. I already felt better. "Should we take out the boat?" One of the girls asked, and everyone nodded in agreement. So, we all got on our swimsuits, lathered on some sunscreen, and headed out for a fun day on the water.

We were having an amazing time when a group of guys in another boat pulled up next to us. They were friendly and we all made small talk, then I noticed a pair of jet skis on the back of their boat. "Jet skis? That's awesome. I've never been on a jet ski before."

One of the guys caught my eye. "Want to give it a try?"

"Really?" They were shiny, looked brand new, and I was curious. "Sure!"

"Alright!" he yelled. "Come on over!"

My friends laughed in delight, and I went over to try out the jet ski. He got on first, and I sat behind him with my arms around his waist. "Ready?" he asked.

"Ready!"

With that, he took off. I didn't know anything about jet skis, but I knew he was going fast, too fast. He shot through the water, whipping around, taking tight turns, and all I could do was try to hold on. Then without any warning, he swerved sharply to the right, sending me flying. I slammed into the water with so much force I felt like I had landed on concrete. I had fallen right on my ribs and the wind was knocked out of me. He circled back around. "Sorry about that. Are you alright?"

"I don't know," I managed. I couldn't breathe deeply, and I could barely speak. Shakily I climbed back on and he brought me to my friends, but my fun weekend getaway had just turned into a nightmare. The pains in my ribs were stabbing and a million different questions flooded through my mind. How would this affect my swimming career? How badly was I injured? What if I couldn't compete? This was the one weekend I had to get away from swimming and do something for myself. I had come to St. Petersburg to rest and get away from my problems, not to create more.

"How much does it hurt?" one of the girls asked.

"Not so bad," I said, wincing in pain.

My friends, being the incredible friends they were, insisted that we drive back to Gainesville that night. "There's no way we're staying. You can't even talk. We've got to get you to a doctor as soon as possible."

We drove back to the University of Florida that night and before I knew it, what I had hoped would be a whimsical weekend was over and I was left in excruciating pain. The next day was Sunday and none of the clinics were open. I called my trainer, and she agreed to meet me at one of the athletic facilities on campus. The pain was so severe that the night before I hadn't been able to sleep at all, and as she poked and prodded at my ribs I grimaced. She suspected that I had either fractured a rib or punctured something and the next day I went in for an MRI. My trainer was right. I had fractured a rib. I stared at the doctor in disbelief. "What can I do?"

"There's not a whole lot you can do for a fractured rib except for rest, and give it time to heal."

Time to heal? World Trials was exactly one month away and time was not something I had. "Isn't there something you can do to fix it?"

Shaking her head, the doctor didn't seem overly concerned. "Don't worry. You can just take the summer off, and you'll be better by September."

"September? I have World Trials in June. I can't take time off. That's not even an option."

"Oh," she replied. "That may be a problem."

Four weeks was all that stood between me and showing up to compete for a spot on the World Championship Team at World Championship Trials so I never even considered taking a break. I showed up to practice every day, but I couldn't rotate my body or swim with my arms. It hurt to talk, and I had to catch myself whenever I wanted to laugh. My motion was so limited that all I could do was kick. Coach Troy put me in a lane by myself, and every practice I would grab a kickboard. For two hours every single day, twice a day, I kicked in a lane by myself and wore my goggles so that no one could see me cry. My entire body was in tremendous pain, I was dreading World Championship Trials, and I was even less enthusiastic about swimming than I had been before I left for St. Petersburg. I didn't want anyone to know that I was injured, so I only told the people who had to know. But one way or another everyone found out. Despite that I had never spoken about my injury or announced that I was hurt, it was all over the media and swim outlets. The news was that I had peaked, that I was injured, and that there was no way I would qualify for World Championships. Reading everything that I feared most about myself written for the entire world to see made my stomach churn and my heart sink. Needless to say, the news flurry did nothing for my mental state. I had no idea how to overcome what I was feeling. How would I go to World Trials and not embarrass myself or fail my coaches, my university, and my country? Were they right? Was I already a has-been whose career was over?

Coach Troy was amazingly supportive and I would go to his office regularly for encouragement. Sometimes we would even call Chuck and put him on speakerphone, and they both assured me that this one meet didn't define who I was as an athlete. But as I read more and more negative things printed about myself and the future of my swimming career, I wasn't so sure. Finally, a grueling four weeks later, we were on our way to the 2013 World Championship Trials. Because of drug testing, I was only able to take Advil, ice my rib, and hope for the best. I was slated to swim the 400 IM, 200 IM, and 200 backstroke. I wasn't sure how I was going to race, but I was determined to prove to myself and the world that I could still compete. It took every ounce of willpower I had to propel myself through the water, and the pain was so intense that I cried throughout the duration of all three swims. I didn't qualify in the 200 backstroke but I came in second in the 400 IM and the 200 IM, which meant I qualified for the World Championships in both events. My ribs ached deeply once I was finished, but I knew that Trials was the easy part. World Championships is a different beast, and the thought of competing against the best in the world with a fractured rib flooded me with anxiety.

Three weeks after trials, I went to the World Championships in Barcelona, Spain. I still wasn't supposed to swim, but I had never adhered to that anyhow. In the 200 IM, I didn't make the finals, but the 400 IM was my event. I had qualified for the team with a fractured rib, and I had absolutely nothing to lose. That world stage was the place I loved most, and those World Championships evoked everything in me that had been missing since the 2012 London Olympics. As I walked out on the deck for my 400 IM, I heard the crowd roar to life, and I knew in that moment that I had realigned with the sport I loved so much. I almost had swimming taken away from me, and I felt energized and ridiculously grateful to be standing there at the World Championships. I dove in, ignored the pain, and instead of crying, I concentrated on doing my best in each and every leg of the race. I came in third, won a bronze medal, and felt the familiar high that came with victory. I couldn't believe I had let myself sink into such a rut, and I was actually thankful for my fractured rib. It reminded me of how lucky I was to have swimming and how much it meant to me to be able to race. My rib would be better soon, and then I could start training seriously. Suddenly, I wanted to swim again. That was a huge wake-up call for me and that bronze medal was the validation I needed. If I could swim that well when I was injured, what could I accomplish when I was healthy again? Mentally, I was back.

When I was done with Worlds, I went directly to the University of Florida for my senior year. I was stoked. I was relieved to be back in my swimming groove, and my rib was finally healed. Because I knew it was my last year swimming for the Gators, I wanted to do my absolute best. I found myself cherishing every meet and even savoring practice and time with my teammates. Unlike the year before, when I had begrudgingly gone through the motions and drug myself to practice, I appreciated each and every experience that came with my last year of college swimming. Once I was back in the game and ready to give my all, swimming was just as rewarding as it had been before London. I loved showing up to the pool and training, and my strokes and times improved as drastically as my attitude. I had good friends, I was still a straight "A" student, and I had finally worked my way out of the dark cloud that had plagued me for so long. In March of my senior year, the 2014 NCAA Championships in Indianapolis, Indiana, marked the end of my collegiate swimming career. I felt proud that I had ended on a high note, and I was glad my last year competing for the University of Florida was a good one.

As an NCAA athlete, you are ineligible to swim professionally. But after that meet I was no longer a college swimmer, and I had agents and sponsors contacting me as soon as I got back to campus. I didn't know how to respond to the volume of offers or even evaluate their proposals. Unsure of what to do, Coach Troy came to my aid, as always. "Don't pay an agent," he said. "Let me help you. We'll work on this together." I knew he had done the same for numerous other athletes, and I was bursting with joy when I ended up signing a four-year contract with Speedo. Everyone in the swimming world knows Speedo, and it had been my favorite swimwear company since I was a little girl. I had pranced around in their bathing suits, plastered their posters around my room, and looked up to all the swimmers who represented their brand. I couldn't believe I was going to be a Speedo athlete and that they were going to pay me to do what I loved most, swim.

It was literally a dream come true. I got paid to go to photo shoots, travel for appearances, and although I was still swimming within the same circle of meets, I was finally allowed to accept prize money when I won. I loved professional swimming. The summer of 2014 was one of the best summers of my life. I went to Nationals and qualified for Pan Pacific Championships in the 200 backstroke and the 400 IM. That year Pan Pacs took place in Australia, which meant I got to travel across the world for the meet and won gold in the 400 IM and bronze in the 200 backstroke. Not only did I get medals and prize money but I had secured myself a spot in World Championships the following year. I was high on life. I was a Speedo athlete, back on my game, loving swimming, and I was doing better than I had hoped in competitions. I followed up that summer with the FINA Swimming World Cup Series in the fall and got to race in Beijing, Tokyo, and Singapore. I couldn't get over the fact that every time I won, they handed me cash. It was unbelievable. I was done with school, making money, traveling the world, and I was winning. Life was good.

After a phenomenal summer and fall of competing, I went to a Grand Prix meet in Austin, Texas, in January 2015. On Saturday afternoon, I dove in for my 400 IM as usual, but somewhere during the 100 breaststroke I heard a distinct snap in my left leg. The second I got out of the water, I went to find Coach Troy. "Something's wrong." I told him what had happened. "I don't know what I did but I'm nervous. I heard a pop."

"Don't worry," he said after pacing for a few minutes. "Maybe it's nothing. Just go to sleep tonight, and see how it feels in the morning."

I did as Coach Troy said and hoped that the next day everything would be fine. But on Sunday morning when I woke up and went to the pool, I literally couldn't even swim breaststroke. The movement created a terrible pain on the inside of my leg, and I later found out that I had pulled my groin. I was livid. Another injury? Until that point, professional swimming couldn't have gone better. I was happy, healthy, and there wasn't anything else I'd rather be doing. But I didn't know what another injury would mean now that I swam professionally. My livelihood literally depended on my being physically able to compete. I didn't want to let down Speedo, and I had already qualified for Worlds.

There was no way I could just take a break; I had to train. So, I pretended nothing was wrong and went right on swimming. I took zero time off and because I didn't let my body recover, I ended up tearing a muscle in my outer leg called the vastus lateralis. My trainer warned me that I should rest for a month, but I refused to take even one day off. Now, not only did I still have the groin injury, but I also had torn the muscle on the same leg because I had been overcompensating due to the pain. I had been able to swim through my fractured rib, but swimming through a torn muscle was not an option. I couldn't train the way I needed to, and I started gaining weight. I wasn't at my best, and with each day that I wasn't able to change that, my spirits dropped lower. I found myself plummeting into a downward spiral. I was a swimmer. That's who I had always been. Since I was seven years old that's ultimately how I had defined myself, and I hadn't ever really questioned that before. But during those seven months, I couldn't help but wonder who I was without swimming. Did I even know? I was afraid of the answer.

I went to the World Championships that year, and it was the first time in any international meet that I didn't even make the finals in one event. That was the most embarrassing moment of my life. Worlds were held in Russia, and my entire family had flown in just to watch me lose. I was so ashamed. I had let down myself, my family, my country, my teammates, and my coaches. I had a duty to represent the USA and I had a job to do for Speedo, and there was no doubt that I had failed miserably at both. I hated myself for that. After that meet, I couldn't even look at myself in the mirror. It was my rock bottom. There was nothing Coach Troy, my parents, Chuck, or even Danny could say to make it better, and all I wanted was to disappear. Coach Troy found me after the competition and looked me dead in the eye. "You've got a choice. You either rise to the occasion of the Olympics or this is it for you and your swimming career. But you need to make a decision right now. We're a year away from the Olympics. You're either in or you're out."

CHAPTER SIXTEEN

After Worlds, we headed directly to the Colorado Springs Olympic Training Center. Because the Olympics were a year away, we hit the ground running. There was no break or time to let up if we wanted to be our best for trials. I was far from over my humiliating loss at Worlds, but deep down I knew I would always regret it if I didn't train for the Olympics one more time. My dream was to win gold, and I had come so close in London. If I gave up now, I would never be the Olympic champion I had always wanted to become. With my performance at the World Championships, quitting seemed to make sense. But I wanted that gold medal more than I had ever wanted anything, and even though the odds were stacked against me, I had to at least try. Coach Troy came up to me while we were in Colorado. "You just had the worst year of swimming in your life. We're going to turn this around." That was exactly what I wanted to do.

"It's an Olympic year, and we're hitting the ground running. We're not waiting until the last minute to put our work in, we're doing it now. And we're going to be ready for Rio in 2016," Coach Troy declared. Starting with our time at the Olympic Training Center, I was grinding. I showed up early for practice and stayed late. I was eating right, going to bed early, and determined to battle my way back to being one of the best swimmers in the world. I spent September through January in Gainesville. I didn't go home for Thanksgiving, and I only went back to Rhode Island for four days at Christmas. It was do or die. I had no choice. I couldn't have another meet like my last World Championships. We attended a competition in January of 2016 that marked six months from Olympic Trials. It was just a small meet in Orlando that we drove down for as a team, and I hoped that all of the training and hard work I had put in would pay off. But when I dove in, my times not only hadn't improved, they had actually gotten worse. I didn't understand. When it came to preparation there was literally nothing else I could have done. I was burnt out.

I knew from how I felt during my races that my times weren't going to be great. Normally when I race, my brain shuts off completely and I go into another underwater world. Coach Troy always said that's why I was such a good racer. I was able to block out every single distraction and factor that could potentially affect my swim when it came time to race. Usually the only thing on my mind when I was in the water was touching the wall first. But at 23, I had started to wonder what a life without swimming looked like. The joy the water used to bring me just wasn't there. In fact, without swimming everything I had to worry about on a daily basis would be over. I wouldn't have to be so incessantly regimented about how much rest I was getting, what I ate, and how I trained. I wouldn't have to obsess over the times I was making or not making at practice and the pressure of winning medals and races to ensure I got a paycheck would be over. Besides, I was sick of the constant aches and pains that came with pushing my body to the max day in and day out. Suddenly, life after swimming didn't look so bad. And that was where my mind was during that meet. Not in the pool, but focused on what I could do outside of it. I had expected my times to be a second or two slower because of my mental state. But when I finished my races and saw the results, I was adding close to ten seconds in every event. When we got back to Gainesville, I scheduled a meeting with Coach Troy.

I sat down across from him in the same office where he had first asked me if I wanted to be an Olympic champion. For the first time in my entire life, the answer to that question had changed. "I want to quit."

Coach Troy's eyes narrowed. "You want to what?"

"Listen, everything they wrote about me before Worlds, maybe they were right. I've peaked. I'm training as hard as I possibly can. I'm eating right; I'm treating my body the best I ever have, and I'm not getting any better. I'm showing up in every way I can, and I'm only getting worse. I can't do it anymore. It's not worth it to me." It was the only time I had ever even talked about quitting swimming and as much as the thought scared me, I didn't see how I could succeed.

"You're really going to quit six months out of the Olympic trials after everything you've been through? Now? You're just going to give it all up?" Coach Troy asked incredulously.

"You've seen how I'm swimming. How am I supposed to be the best in the world in six months? Tell me how."

Coach Troy leaned forward. "Elizabeth, every single time you show up to practice, it's like putting money in the bank. The more money you have in the bank at the end of the season, the better off you are. Whether it shows up now or later, you coming to practice and working hard is only going to help you. It's January, you've got time. Don't quit now. At least give yourself a shot. See how much money you've got in your bank come Olympic Trials. If you don't make the USA Team, at least you'll be able to sleep at night knowing that you tried. You still want to quit, that's fine. But my advice to you is to stick it out, be tough, and keep putting money in your bank. Think it over."

I didn't come to practice for the next three days. The truth was I didn't want to quit, I wanted to be the best. But I was torn between what I wanted and what I thought was realistic. I was still thrown from my less than stellar meet in Orlando, and I couldn't train any harder. If I wasn't going to be able to improve, I didn't see the point. Part of me was ready to be done, but in the end, the goal of winning a gold medal was enough to drive me back. I showed up to practice four days after our conversation and walked up to Coach Troy. "I thought about what you said. Let's do this." From that moment on, a switch flipped. I started having more fun and then, finally, my times started to get faster. That May I went to a tune-up meet at Georgia

Tech's pool in Atlanta, which was the site of the 1996 Olympic Games. The meet was casual; there was no prize money involved or media hype, and that also meant no pressure. The meet was essentially an opportunity for swimmers to race and work on techniques, race strategies, and splits. There was a decent number of Olympians at the meet competing but we were all there for the same reason—not to go fast but to work on our form and strategy before trials. I wasn't rested or prepared, and it was just a 45-minute flight from Gainesville so I had no expectations. I was still waiting to see how much money would show up in my bank before Olympic Trials.

I was reluctant to get my hopes up after World Championships and the brick wall I had previously hit in training, but I felt strong before the 400 IM and like maybe I was once again ready to hardcore race. I just wanted to swim decently so I could get my confidence back when it came to competing. Standing behind the blocks, I shook out my arms and focused on swimming my best. I dove in, and everything felt on. My pace had returned and so had my strength. The difficult training, eating right, and showing up to practice finally felt like it was paying off. When I finished that race, I knew I had money in my bank, I just didn't realize how much. I surprised the swimming community and myself and went the third fastest time in the world. I was psyched. I knew that if I could put up a time like that dead tired, not shaved, and not tapered, I could win a gold medal that summer—so did the media. Suddenly the tide had changed. "Elizabeth Beisel is on fire!" "She's the favorite for gold in Rio." "Watch out for Beisel, she's back."

I was thrilled, and Coach Troy was proud of what I had accomplished which meant the world to me. I was swimming my best times ever, and after all of the struggles, injuries, and challenges, I was back on top. A month out of trials, I was exactly where I was supposed to be and I had no doubt that I would make my third Olympic team. But about 10 days before trials, I woke up and something was off. My head felt fuzzy, my body was achy, and I couldn't keep anything down. I went to the doctor and learned that I had a severe stomach virus. There was nothing they could do except try to keep me hydrated, and I spent four nights and five days in the hospital. Coach Troy didn't want anyone to know I was sick. He was worried the negative press would affect me and my competitors would think they had a leg up. So I didn't tell anyone. During my stay in the hospital I was so sick that I couldn't eat, I didn't sleep, there was no way I could even think about swimming, and I lost eight pounds of muscle. I went from knowing that I would make the Olympic team to not even being able to fathom being well enough to go to trials. But when I finally got better, Coach Troy insisted. "You have your flight booked. You're not dead. You're going to the Olympic Trials."

Four days after I got out of the hospital, I flew to the Olympic Trials in Omaha, Nebraska. From the time I was released from the hospital until my first race, I had six days. While everyone else had enjoyed tapering and was coming in fresh and rested, I still couldn't even keep food down. The hardest day of my entire life was when I had to swim the 400 IM at trials. I had hoped to go in trained, strong, motivated, and ready. But I was still weak and my confidence after being sick had taken a nosedive. I was supposed to be at my best, but physically I felt awful and mentally I was a mess. There was no way I could make the team under those circumstances.

I dove in for warm-ups and hoped that somehow the water would wash everything away and make me feel better, but it didn't. When prelims came, I swam my very hardest and miraculously made finals—although, I have no idea how. I spent the entirety of that afternoon crying hysterically. I couldn't eat, I felt terrible, and I knew that when it came to the Olympics this was my last chance. If I didn't qualify in the 400 IM that night, I would never win a gold medal. I had devoted so much time and effort to making that dream happen, that thinking about having it taken away was heartbreaking. Laura and Schmitty literally held me. I was sobbing so hard that my entire body was convulsing. They didn't leave my side and both of them were so supportive and positive. "Beisel, you've got this!" "You've done it once, you've done it twice, you can do it again." "You're the one they're all scared of." Without Laura and Schmitty, I don't know what I would have done, and even now, I would never wish to relive that day.

When I got to the pool that night, I had no idea what would happen. I wasn't sure I was even capable of completing a 400 IM, much less doing so against the best swimmers in the country. I thought back to the last four years of my life. Everything had been working up towards that one moment, so that I could make the Olympic team, and go for gold. If I didn't qualify, the last four years would all be for nothing. When I got in to warm-up, I didn't speak to anyone and I couldn't find my rhythm in the water. After a few laps, I touched the wall and saw Coach Troy standing over me. "What's going on? Get out, and talk to me."

I climbed out of the pool and before he could say another word, I started crying all over again. "There's no way I'm going to make the team tonight. I can't do this." The amount of pain and agony I was in was unbearable.

"Look, you already made finals." He grabbed my hands. "Elizabeth, you've got more money in the bank than anyone you're racing against. You have to believe that. You have to believe you can do this. Because if you don't, you're not going to make the team and all of those practices you worked so hard, all of those hours you dedicated and sacrificed won't matter. Do it for yourself tonight. It's going to be the hardest 400 IM of your life, but you're going to be so happy when it's over. Because you will make that Olympic team tonight. I know you will." After that Coach Troy left me to my thoughts.

I didn't necessarily have confidence in myself at that moment, but I did believe in Coach Troy. When it came to finals that night, he was right. It was the hardest 400 IM I had ever swum both mentally and physically because so much was on the line. I fought for every single stroke up and down the pool during those 400 meters, and my body screamed in pain as I pushed to my threshold. The entire race felt like I was trying desperately to sprint through water as thick and sticky as molasses, but when I finally hit the wall, I finished second and qualified for my third Olympic Games.

I came in second to Maya DiRado who had just qualified for her first Olympic Team. On her face was disbelief and complete joy, which I recognized from when I had first qualified for the 2008 Beijing Olympic Games. I knew that smile and exactly what it felt like to finally make that first team. While Maya was overjoyed, I was quite simply enormously relieved. The first time you qualify for the Olympics is the most amazing moment there is, because it's never an expectation the first time around. It might be likely, but it doesn't come with the amount of pressure that automatically is applied to returning Olympians. Had I not been sick, the pressure of showing up at trials and trying to make my third Olympics would have been immense. Given the circumstances, it was almost catastrophic, and I never wanted to feel the way I felt that day again. I was so tired after that race I could barely even catch my breath enough to congratulate Maya. But I was happy for her and proud to welcome her to Team USA.

When I was done with the race, I went through mixed zones. I felt like I was going to fall over I was so exhausted, and I had to concentrate extra hard in order to provide the reporters with sufficient answers to their questions. Finally, I exited the pool deck and Coach Troy was the first person I saw. I immediately ran to him, wrapped my arms around his shoulders, and we both started crying uncontrollably. Making that Olympic team was the most difficult thing I've ever done, but the race was over and I was going to Rio.

CHAPTER SEVENTEEN

Once the 400 IM was finished, I was free to focus on the rest of the meet. I was getting stronger, feeling better, and I was finally able to eat again. After three days, I was back in the water and ready to swim the 200 backstroke. When I was warming up for prelims, I was relieved to find that I once again felt like myself in the water. At least I did until I collided with another swimmer. I was doing a breakout stroke, and another swimmer and I hit hands. Warm-ups at big meets are often chaotic, and it's not abnormal to graze someone in another lane. Usually you shake it off and just keep going, but I could barely even make it to the other end of the pool. I got out and looked everywhere for Coach Troy, but I couldn't find him. Then I ran into Chuck. "Chuck! My hand just got nailed, and there's something wrong. I can't even swim and I don't know what to do."

"Don't worry. Let's look around for Troy."

Once we finally found Coach Troy it was only 30 minutes before my race. "There's no time," he said. "You're going to have to suck it up and make it to semis, and then we'll figure it out." I couldn't believe it. After my stomach virus, now this? I sat in the ready room, my hand throbbing, with my goggles on so no one could see me cry. It took me back to my days of kick boarding when I had fractured my rib and had used the same strategy to conceal my tears during practice. Had I really overcome that much and made it that far just for something else to go wrong at the very worst possible time? My only focus was on doing my best, and I relied on muscle memory to get me through. I had raced the 200 backstroke so many times before; I just had to make it to semi-finals, and then I could take care of my hand. I swam in prelims and made semis, then went to find Coach Troy again. "Look, Elizabeth" Coach Troy said. "If it's really that bad I can't take you to the emergency room right now. But Chuck can." Coach Troy still had swimmers with events that day, but since Chuck didn't, he had volunteered to take me to the ER. Finals were that night and less than five hours away, so I didn't even change out of my racing suit. I grabbed my parka, and Chuck whizzed me over to the emergency room. Sitting in the waiting room, soaking wet in my skin tight racing suit and oversized parka, people stared at me like I was crazy, but Chuck stayed with me the entire time.

Words couldn't describe what I was feeling sitting there. I had beaten all odds to qualify in the 400 IM after being in the hospital the week before, and now I was in the emergency room literally hours before my next qualifying race. I was angry and frustrated to the nth degree. I had trained so hard and given up so much. Was it too much to ask just to be healthy for trials?

Finally, it was my turn and we went back to see the doctor. A quick MRI showed that I had fractured my finger. Seriously? The doctor stared at my racing suit. "Well at least you're done. You don't have to swim anytime soon, right?"

"No," I said. "I'm swimming tonight." And it wasn't just any swim, it was the Olympic trials. How could this be happening?

"I wouldn't recommend doing that," he replied.

"Well, I have to. So, what can I do?"

He shrugged. I couldn't take any medication because of drug testing so he gave me a shot in my hand to numb the pain. But when I saw the huge needle pierce through my skin, everything went white, and when I opened my eyes again, I was on the floor and Chuck was looking down at me. "It's okay. Take your time getting up. You just fainted."

Lying on the floor of the emergency room in my racing suit and swim parka with a broken finger was not how I had envisioned trials. The doctor offered one more suggestion, and that was to buddy tape my finger. It was my pinkie finger that was fractured, so I could tape it to my ring finger, but there wasn't anything else he could do. Great. After we left, Chuck took me to grab food at Jimmy John's and then we went back to the hotel. I only had a couple of hours until I had to be ready for warm-ups, and as I laid down to rest, I realized that my hand was still completely numb. Not only was it uncomfortable, but if the shot didn't wear off, I wouldn't be able to feel the water. I wasn't able to sleep at all before I had to get back to the pool for my race. That night, when I dove in for warm-ups, I still had no feeling in my hand. There was no way to tell how much water I was holding, which is essential for swimming. I couldn't even register when my hand was hitting the pool, and my pace was awful. Before I left for the ready room Coach Troy found me. "Don't worry. At this point, you've already made the team. Swim with your fingers buddy taped, and just do the best you can. Yes, I want you to make backstroke but if you don't it doesn't matter. You've already got your ticket punched to Rio. You're going to the Olympics either way."

Coach Troy was right, but I already felt defeated. I was okay with not making the Olympic team in either event if I couldn't put up the times. I still would have been horrifically upset and disappointed, but I would have had peace of mind in knowing that I had left everything in the pool. What killed me was that I wasn't able to do my best. I had pulled out a victory in the 400 IM after my stomach virus, and now a fractured finger just seemed unfair. I didn't want to lose because of a freak accident in warm-ups. But I had no choice but to dive in and swim. After I buddy-taped my fingers, I was ready for semi-finals. The race was awkward and I felt totally off center the entire time, but I made it to finals. I climbed out of the pool, and before I could leave the deck an official came up to me. "I'm so sorry to tell you this, but we're going to have to disqualify you."

If I had thought that day couldn't get worse, I was wrong. "What? Why?"

"Your fingers can't be buddy-taped. The problem is if they are, that creates a paddle and having a paddle in swimming when you race is illegal."

My eyes teared up, and I wanted to scream every single cuss word imaginable. I knew what a paddle was and having two fingers taped together on my hand that was still numb most certainly wasn't one. After fracturing my finger that day, fainting, and not even being able to have a feel for the water in my race, they thought this was an advantage? I knew the situation wasn't something I could handle on my own, so I immediately found Coach Troy and Chuck. "They said I'm disqualified."

"What?" Coach Troy and Chuck were outraged when I told them that the officials thought buddy taping my fingers was a valid reason for a DQ. "This isn't happening," Coach Troy said, and they both stormed off.

Ultimately, the disqualification was appealed, but I wasn't allowed to buddy tape my fingers for finals. I kept the tape on for warm-ups, and untaped my fingers right behind the blocks before my race. I was exhausted and fed up with my unbelievably bad luck. I was so sick of that meet, and the only thing I wanted was to get out of Omaha. I didn't want to be there anymore, and that was how I swam my race in 200 backstroke final at the 2016 Olympic Trials. I didn't qualify for 200 backstroke and I didn't even care. Mentally, I had completely shut down. I was fed up with swimming and everything the Universe had thrown at me. I didn't understand. Why me? I had put in so much time and effort and worked through so much over the course of the last four years to make that the summer of Elizabeth Beisel, and it had all come crashing down on me within a two-week span of time.

CHAPTER EIGHTEEN

My favorite headline going into the 2016 Olympic Trials was when the media had printed that I was on fire and the one to beat. That was how I felt. I had put everything I had into my practices, upped my training, meticulously ate a healthy diet, and did everything else within my power to prepare. But by the end of trials, the flames I had spent four years fanning were out. I had barely qualified in my best event. Leading up to trials, I hadn't even considered that I might not make it in the 200 backstroke. And it wasn't that I choked. That I could have owned. It was that I could have done better if I had just been 100 percent. Now, I was going to Rio with a fractured finger that wouldn't be healed for another six months. The Olympics is literally the fiercest competition in the world, and I was walking in with a disadvantage. Having your hand healthy in swimming is huge because that's how you hold water. And with my injury I wasn't able to perform at my peak. It felt like the Universe had beaten me down, and all I could do was throw up my arms in defeat. I had sacrificed so much up until that point, and after trials I knew in my heart of hearts, that I wasn't going to win gold. All of the expectations and drive and excitement that had continuously built momentum before trials vanished overnight.

I was once again part of Team USA and I wanted to make the best of things, but everything that had happened still rested heavy on my mind. Once trials were over, we flew to a camp in San Antonio to train. Afterwards we were supposed to go to Puerto Rico, but due to hurricanes, we had to be relocated. We ended up flying to Atlanta, Georgia, instead, and slowly I began to feel better. I was rooming with Schmitty and honored to be going to the Olympics for my third time. But I was also frustrated. My finger still hurt every day, and I wasn't able to reach my usual pace times in practice. While I enjoyed the atmosphere and the other swimmers, I couldn't get my head back in the game swimming-wise. The truth is I had decided I wasn't going to win before we ever flew to Rio. I hated myself for that, and I tried to talk myself out of that mindset every possible way I could. But no matter what I did or how hard I tried to turn it around, I had a sinking feeling that it wasn't going to be my summer.

When we got to Rio, the city was booming with the excitement of the Olympics. It felt right to be back, rooming with Schmitty, in a city taken over by the enthusiasm and enormity of the Olympic Games. Rio wasn't portrayed in the most flattering light prior to the Olympics, but I found the city to be beautiful, friendly, and charming. Located right on the beach, I was at home being near the ocean. Large palm trees populated the paths throughout the village, and that coupled with sunshine, made every day look like paradise. All of the apartments where we were staying were painted bright vibrant colors and there were large inviting lounge pools in nearly every courtyard. Latin music played on loudspeakers throughout the village, making everything seem more festive, and the locals were willing to go above and beyond to make us feel welcome. Each of our rooms had a spacious balcony overlooking the rest of the village, and we were able to keep the doors open and let the fresh air breeze through our apartments. The dining hall had a distinct South American influence and an endless array of options, and I loved everything about the city.

Even if I wasn't particularly thrilled with the swimming part up until that point, it was amazing and humbling to be at my third Olympic Games. In fact, I found myself in a position where the younger members of the team were now looking to me for guidance. The swimmers who were new to the team were asking me for advice and coming to me when they were uncertain about what to expect. I recognized the eager excitement and nervous uncertainty all too well.

At my first Olympics in Beijing, I had been an awkward 15-year-old. Now, at 23, I was the veteran third time Olympian. I liked that role, and even if I didn't feel confident about my own swimming, I was more than happy to help the younger swimmers just like so many people had helped me along the way.

As usual, about a week before the meet started, we voted on team captains. I was ecstatic when I found out later that night that I been elected as one of the USA Olympic Team captains. To me, that was one of the biggest honors of my life. I was so proud my teammates had voted for me and that gave me a renewed sense of duty in Rio. The additional two women captains were Allison Schmitt and Camille Adams, and the men were Michael Phelps, Nathan Adrian, and Anthony Ervin. I was in exceptional company when it came to the other team captains, and I took that responsibility very seriously. I was going to be there for my teammates just as older members of the team had always been there for me. I wasn't going to be the Michael Phelps of the team or the face of USA Swimming that Olympics, but I was okay with being the one helping everyone else bring home medals.

The day of my race, I knew I was not going to win. I was also well aware that my mentality really sucked. But I still couldn't talk myself out of the negative thoughts which had been circling through my mind since trials. I went into prelims, and the only thing I kept telling myself was that I just wanted to make it to finals. I had never swum like that, especially not at the Olympic Games. I knew that was a red flag, but to my own detriment, I couldn't flip things around in my mind. I was one of the best 400 IMers in the world. A few months ago, I had been the one to beat. But I wasn't that day, and I just wanted my race to be over. It was such an internal battle. I knew I should desperately want to win gold, but truthfully, I had given up on that race long before I jumped in the pool. As much of a difference as it had made when I was able to believe in myself before a meet, not being able to muster a sense of confidence in my own ability was equally debilitating. I swam prelims, and I did make it to finals but I qualified fourth. Every Olympics I had qualified first for finals with the one exception of qualifying second for the 200 backstroke in 2008, so qualifying fourth messed with my head even more. I tried to motivate myself, awaken that competitive drive and spark the fiery ambition that had gotten me through the last four years, but after trials, it just wasn't there.

Once I finished my race, I went to the warm-down pool, still struggling with how to force myself to actually want to compete and I ran into Michael Phelps. I could tell by the look on his face that he knew I wasn't okay. I walked up to him and collapsed into his arms. "I know" he said. "Trust me I know exactly how you feel." He was in a similar position four years ago during London, and he and I had discussions prior about how hard his last Olympics had been. "But you've been here before," he continued. "This is your third time. And you know you can do it tonight. You have one more swim. That's it. Just one more swim. Give it everything you've got. That's all you have to do." I tried with all of my might to hold onto his words and make myself believe them. But I didn't. I spent that entire afternoon completely complacent. I wasn't nervous or excited. I just sat in our apartment, staring blankly ahead.

Schmitty wasn't racing that day, and she did her best to build me up. "Are you pumped for tonight?"

"Not really," I said.

"Can I do anything for you? What do you need? Anything. You've got it. Please let me do something for you."

I shook my head. "Schmitty, this is just it. I have one race, and it's not going to go the way I want it."

"You don't know that!" She said, trying to cheer me up.

But deep down I did. I had decided that before we even flew to Rio, and no matter how badly I wanted to turn my pessimistic view around, I still hadn't. I wasn't going to win gold. I was going to be lucky if I won a medal at all. As I sat in the ready room, all I cared about was that I wasn't last in my heat. I had gone from being absolutely certain I would win gold to just wanting my swim to be over. It was my last Olympic race, and I'd be lying if I said I left everything I had in the pool. Or maybe I did. But I didn't have very much to give that night. Either way, I came in sixth. It was a far cry from what I had hoped for before trials had bulldozed over my high expectations for the 2016 Olympics. When I got out of the pool, I walked through the mixed zone and not a single person interviewed me. The people who had projected me as the favorite for gold didn't even say a quick hello or how do you feel when I came in sixth. I didn't have to fake being happy for the cameras because nobody cared.

I didn't talk to anyone. I went straight to the locker room, sat down in the shower, and cried. It was such a mixture of emotions. I felt relief because it was over, failure because I had done so poorly, sadness because I knew it my last Olympics, and an overwhelming sense of regret that I was worried I'd never be able to shake. That's not how my last Olympics was supposed to go. I had done so much to ensure that I was able to compete the way I wanted to in Rio, but I had fallen short. The last four years felt like a never-ending uphill battle. Every time I overcame one setback, another had appeared in its place. I had always kept going because I wanted to be an Olympic champion so badly, but all I had to show for everything I had been through was a sixth place finish. I don't think I've ever felt lower than I did, sitting in that shower in Brazil, knowing that the dream I had been chasing all of my life was now gone. I had just given up my chance to win gold and the weight of that realization was crushing. But after I was finished crying, I knew I had two choices. I could spend the rest of the Olympics feeling sorry for myself, moping around, and obsessing over something I couldn't change, or I could rise to the occasion. I could be the leader I was elected to be and make sure that my teammates had the best experience possible. I wasn't going to contribute to the team with medals, but I owed it to everyone who helped me along the way to do the same for the other swimmers. So, I made a decision. I would put a smile on my face no matter how hard it was, and I would be there for my team. I would spend the rest of the Olympics having a blast, cheering on the United States, and trying to enjoy every single moment because I knew I would never experience an Olympic Games from that point of view again.

After that race, my Olympic career was over. I knew it, my family knew it, and so did Coach Troy. When I finally left the locker room and was able to face that, I swam for 20 straight minutes in the warm down pool. I knew I would never have the opportunity to swim at an Olympic venue again, and being in the water helped me clear my head. When I got out and went to find Troy, he knew exactly what I needed. He didn't review my splits with me, and we didn't go over what I could have done better. Instead, he engulfed me in a huge bear hug. "I know how hard making it here was, and I know that last race wasn't easy. But I'm so proud of you."

There's an Olympic creed, which is a cornerstone of any Games. "The most important thing in the Olympic Games is not to win but to take part, just as the most important thing in life is not the triumph but the struggle. The essential thing is not to have conquered but to have fought well." It's a quote which is attributed to Pierre de Coubertin and when Coach Troy finally released me, he wasn't frowning in disappointment, he was smiling. "You lived up to the Olympic creed tonight, and you have in every race you've ever competed in at the Olympics. That's something far more important than winning a medal." I was beyond relieved to hear Coach Troy say those words. All of my teammates gave me big hugs, and I went to find Maya, who had won her first Olympic silver medal in the 400 IM, so that I could congratulate her.

After that day, I held true to my decision. I spent the rest of my time in Rio helping out my team in any and every way possible and appreciating the Olympics. There were small things, like savoring wearing my Team USA clothes as an athlete and smiling to myself every time I noticed the prominent five rings that I had seen for the first time on television in my living room. But there were larger moments too. I recognized that I could be the person who I had needed when I was younger. I had come full circle and just like Natalie Coughlin, Teresa Crippen, Margaret Hoelzer, and my big brother Ryan had come through for me, I found a great sense of pride in being a pillar of support for the less experienced members of the team.

One of the highlights of that Olympics for me was seeing one of my best friends and training partners, Caeleb Dressel, and other new swimmers get to experience their very first Olympic Games. It was touching to see the Olympic Games through their point of view, where everything was brand new, overwhelmingly intense, and awe-inspiring. It reminded me of what an amazing accomplishment it was to even make the Olympics at all, and it also made me appreciate the rest of my time in Rio that much more. Caeleb swam with me at the University of Florida, and he was still a teenager and beyond thrilled to be a part of Team USA. He's an incredibly hard worker, always positive, and one of the most genuine humans on the planet, so I wanted more than anything for him to do well. The day of his race, he was ridiculously nervous. "I can't believe we're here at the Olympics."

I laughed. I liked how much he appreciated the novelty of being part of Team USA. "You've swum this a million times before, and it's no different than any other pool," I assured him.

Caeleb stared at me then up at the stands. "Except there's like the entire world watching."

"Don't think about that. You're going to be fine. In fact, you're going to do more than that. I think you're going to win."

"Really?"

"Absolutely." His first race was the 400 freestyle relay, and I knew they had a good shot at the gold. I stayed with him throughout his entire warm up. I wanted to make sure he was okay and that his nerves didn't get the best of him. When I finally left him to go up to the competition stands, I think I was as nervous as he was. "Good luck. You've got this."

When I sat down with a few fellow team members to see the race, I could hardly sit still. I wanted Caeleb to win a medal so badly. I had seen how hard he trained, and the amount of work he did every single day, and I knew how much winning a gold medal would mean to him. When they walked out, I was so proud of him. But I could barely keep my eyes on the race. I almost had to look away a few times when the competition got a little too close. "Go! Go!" I screamed at the very top of my lungs. When he touched the wall first, I couldn't contain myself. I burst into tears. It was Caeleb's lifelong dream to win gold, and to be in the stands and see him accomplish that is still a moment that gives me chills.

After that race, every single session, I was in the front row waving an American flag. Seeing a familiar face right before you go off the blocks, before what is ultimately one of the most important races of your life, is comforting. And every time any of our swimmers looked up at the stands, I wanted them to know that someone was cheering them on. I also made a rule. Unfortunately, not everyone is going to have the meet they want at the Olympics. So, I made it known that if anyone had a bad race, they dealt with it with me in the locker room. I wanted everyone to have the best meet possible and that meant not unloading negative energy on the team no matter what happened. We were still there representing the USA, and that was bigger than ourselves. I thrived as a team captain, and to be honest, I was proud of the role I was able to play. We ended up having the most successful Olympic Games in US history that summer. We won more medals than ever before, and being elected team captain saved that Olympics for me. It gave me a purpose—something that after those Olympic Games, I wouldn't easily find again.

CHAPTER NINETEEN

For as long as I could remember, the only thing I ever wanted was to swim. Before I even understood what swimming was, I craved the water, and I had spent my entire life training to win gold. I ended Rio on a good note as a Captain, and I was happy I was able to support my team. But when I got home, I was lost. I moved from Gainesville back into my parents' house in Rhode Island. I told my family that I didn't want any big festivities like after Beijing and London, and I was serious. Sixth place was nothing to celebrate. I had held it together during the games, but when I got home, I broke down. I didn't leave the house because I knew I would be recognized, and I spent most days, sitting solemnly doing nothing. So many people had expected me to be the Olympic gold medalist that year, myself included, and I had failed. There were signs up all over, cheering me on, and that made it even worse. The state of Rhode Island was still behind me, and I didn't want to face anyone because I knew I hadn't delivered.

About a week and a half after I got home, Schmitty called. "I can't do this," she said. Schmitty was probably the only person in the world who knew exactly how I felt. Despite medaling five times in the 2012 London Olympics, she had only medaled once in a relay for Rio, and she was every bit as devastated as I was as a result.

"I know what you mean," I conceded. "But I don't know what to say."

"I think we need to take a trip and get away for a while."

I didn't even ask when, where, or how long. "I'm in."

We ended up booking a one-month trip to Australia and Thailand. I was so grateful to be able to spend time with Schmitty, and we both were more than willing to throw ourselves into the escapism travel offered. During the days, we were distracted with breathtaking scenery, impromptu adventures, and meeting new people. But at night, we often confided in one another about how deeply disappointed we were with our performances in Rio. We both agreed on two things; we had failed irredeemably, and we would never swim again. The sport we both used to love, we now hated, but the trip was cathartic because we could lean on one another and try to lose ourselves in the foreign surroundings. It was when I went home that things got really bad.

I still had a year and a half left on my Speedo contract, and the plan was that I would train with Chuck at Bluefish in Attleboro. But I refused to swim. I didn't work out. And I had no real life back in Rhode Island. I had gone from constant training, to sitting in my parents' house day after day, pondering where it had all gone wrong. I had spent most of my life staring at a black line at the bottom of a pool so that I could be an Olympic champion. But I wasn't. I had given up everything all for nothing. Before I was even six years old I had begged my parents to swim and ever since that day, it was what I did, what I dreamed about, what I worked for, and maybe somewhere along the line, it had become who I was. Had I made all the wrong decisions? I was so proud when I was able to exercise such discipline during training, but ultimately it had landed me back in my childhood bedroom with no gold medal and no clue what came next.

I fell into a deep, dark depression and for the next eight months I ate whatever I wanted, quit working out altogether, drank if I felt like it, and the only positive thing I did was that occasionally I traveled. I went to visit friends or see people. But that was it. I gained 20 pounds and I stopped trying to figure everything out. I just didn't care. "Why don't you just try to swim?" My mother would plead. "You could see Chuck, and you wouldn't even have to stay the whole practice."

I would freak out. "You don't understand! I hate swimming. You have no idea what I'm going through."

It was the worst eight months of my life, and honestly, after working so hard, for so long, and failing, I didn't think anything would ever get better. I had given up a normal life because I thought I was gifted and driven enough to be the best, and I had ended up a loser. Then in April, I got an email from Speedo. They wrote to me and told me they'd noticed I had not competed since August. They very kindly told me that if I wanted to continue to be a Speedo athlete and earn a salary, I needed to do what they were paying me for and swim. That email was like a dagger. Not only had I lost at the Olympics, I was about to have my status as a Speedo athlete taken away, and rightfully so. I knew after reading those words that I had no choice but to start swimming again. I couldn't put it off any longer; I had to get back in the pool. The thought of even putting on a swimsuit gave me anxiety, and there was only two months until World Trials in June. I had no idea where to even start.

The first person I called was Chase Kalisz. He was also a member of Team USA for the 2016 Olympics and an amazing friend. Throughout the duration of the last eight months, he had never given up trying to get me back into swimming. "I'm not necessarily ready, but I just got an email from Speedo and I've got to swim."

"Finally!"

"I don't know what to do. I've got two months until World Championship Trials."

"Okay," Chase said. "Look, Bob Bowman is having a camp in Colorado for the month of May. You should do it. Start going to Bluefish four or five times a week, try to get back into it, and meet me there. You've got nothing to lose, and I promise you I will be there every step of the way. Just text Bob, and make sure he's okay with you coming."

As soon as I got off the phone I texted Bob Bowman, who coached Schmitty, Michael Phelps, and Chase. "I heard you were having a camp in May and was hoping I could join," I wrote.

Bob texted back immediately and told me he would love to have me. About five minutes later, he texted me again. "Just show up in shape."

Shit. I hadn't trained in eight months, and I had two weeks until I'd be expected to make world class times. The next day I called Coach Troy and he fully supported my decision to go to Colorado and train with Bob. That afternoon, for the first time in a long time, I drove the familiar route to Attleboro, Massachusetts, so that I could practice at Bluefish. When I saw Chuck, I wasn't sure what to say. "Hi."

"Hey, stranger. It's been awhile."

I nodded. "Yeah."

"You ready to practice?"

I wasn't sure, but I knew I needed to get back in the water if I had a shot at being able to perform at all at Worlds. "I'm going to try. I'm thinking about going to Colorado in May to train with Bob Bowman; he's having a camp."

"I think that's a great idea."

"Really?"

Chuck nodded. "Of course. You know you're always welcome to practice here, but I think Colorado might be good for you."

"I'm not sure how this is going to go," I admitted, glancing at the pool.

Chuck couldn't have been kinder. "Look, it's been awhile and that's okay. I'm not going to make you do anything you don't want to do. Get in and practice, do the best you can and if you need to leave, leave."

"Thanks," I appreciated his understanding, and I was ready to bite the bullet and get back in the pool. Because Coach Troy and Chuck were behind my decision to go to Colorado and train with Bob in May, everything was set in motion. When I arrived at camp, I was overweight, embarrassed to even put on a bathing suit, and I came in last in every single set. I was swimming with Olympians who had been training for the past eight months, and at first, it was exhausting. But Bob was incredibly patient and encouraging, and

Chase was there for me 100 percent. Every day he made me laugh and essentially forced me to keep going. "I know it sucks now, but you can do this. You're going to go to World Championships this summer," Chase would say. "I know it." I would just roll my eyes, but at some point during that camp, I fell back in love with swimming—not with relentlessly going for gold, or killing myself to make an interval, but with giving my all and being back in the water. Gradually, I got faster and faster and started to lose weight. And after four weeks, the pain and frustration of the last eight months seemed to be washed clean.

Once camp was over, we flew directly to a meet in California at Santa Clara, which is still one of my favorite pools in the world. It was a part of the "Pro Swim Series" and was particularly popular because of its location. You could win prize money, and California was an easy flight for swimmers from China, Australia, and New Zealand who wanted to compete on an international stage against some of the best American swimmers. After a full eight months off, I was less than optimistic. This was tight competition with some of the top swimmers in the World. I had a feeling it would either make me or break me when it came to my confidence going into World Trials.

The pool was located outdoors, which naturally gave the meet a more relaxed feel and, I wondered how much progress I had actually made during the month of May. There was no doubt I had improved dramatically over the course of my stay in Colorado training with Bob. But in my entire life, I had never gone that long without training. I had no idea what sort of times I was capable of putting up when I actually raced. Going up against the best of the best after such a long break was intimidating, but it was either then or at Worlds, and test-driving the competition seemed like the smarter bet. I was floored when I dove in and got second in the 400 IM. That made me happy. I was progressing in my swimming and having fun doing it. The World Trials were three weeks away, and I knew I wasn't going to make the team. But at least, after that meet, I knew I wouldn't humiliate myself. After California, I flew back to Georgia to train with Chase. He was my rock, and I knew that if I stuck with him I'd be okay. I trained for two weeks in Georgia, then spent a week training in Florida with Coach Troy. When I boarded the plane to World Trials in Indianapolis, Indiana, I was as prepared as possible, given the amount of time I had taken off.

I was only entered in one event, the 400 IM. I knew I would retire after that race and I was ready for the last swim of my career. I had no expectations; I just wanted to swim decently. Before my race, Chuck and Coach Troy had a meeting with me on the pool deck. "This is probably the last 400 IM you're ever going to swim. Have fun," Chuck said.

It felt strange to have such a monumental part of my life coming to an end. "Leave it all in the pool," Coach Troy said. Then he winked at me. "You've got one job to do. Just race."

I thought of all the times both those men had been there for me throughout my swimming career, and when they announced my name to swim, I was beaming. Before I dove in, I stared out at the pool, and as trite as it sounds, the entirety of my career flashed through my mind in large glossy mental snapshots. I remembered when Josh had taken the time to perfect my strokes, and how he had assured me that if I worked hard, one day I could go to the Olympics. At seven years old, I couldn't have possibly grasped the ups and downs that would come with the path I chose to pursue. I pictured the first time I made the Olympic team in the 400 IM out of nowhere. I saw Beijing, London, Rio, and all the places and races and people and pools in between. This was the end, and I was ready.

I took my mark on the blocks and dove in when I heard the familiar beep signaling us to start. I swam fly, back, breast, and I knew that when I transitioned into the 100 of freestyle I was in third. I was dead even with a 16-year-old up and coming swimmer. I used to be that girl, but now I hated her. There was no way I was going to let a 16-year-old beat me in the last race of my career, so I reached down deep and dug hard. We literally went stroke for stroke on that last 100 and when we got to the wall, I out touched her. I had swum the best race I could and that was enough. Leah Smith won and Ella Eastin came in second, and both had just made their first World Championship Team in the 400IM. As my career was ending theirs was just beginning, and I saw the enthusiasm and excitement that I had once felt as my journey as a National swimmer had started. "Congratulations!" I hugged them both. "You're the future of USA Swimming!" I was genuinely happy for them, but when I glanced up at the scoreboard the letters 'DQ' were next to Ella's name. "Ella, look at the scoreboard."

"I know!" She said smiling widely. "I'm going to World Championships!"

"No, Ella. Look at the scoreboard."

I had hoped for Ella's sake the DQ would be overturned. But on her last turn she had come off the wall on her back which was illegal, and the disqualification stood. That meant I was going to World Championships to represent the USA for the 12th year in a row. Those weren't the circumstances under which I would have chosen to make the team, but regardless I was on my way to Worlds in Budapest, Hungary. I had thought my career would end in Indianapolis, but I was going to get to compete on the world stage one last time. I was elected captain of the team along with Katie Meili and again, I took on that role with an enormous sense of responsibility. I spent the entire meet cheering on my teammates, encouraging the other swimmers, and enjoying what I knew would be my last time representing the United States of America. I had thought that about the Olympics the year before, but this was a second chance for me to end my time swimming for the USA on my own terms. After 12 years of competing, it was time, and I was grateful for everything swim had given me.

Coach Troy was there in Hungary, and my entire family had flown to Budapest to see my last swim. The day of my event, I just wanted to make finals that night. Being on that team was the happiest

I had ever been, and if I could end my career as one of the top eight in the world that would be an amazing way to go out. I qualified third during prelims and was able to sleep all afternoon. I arrived at the pool for finals that night, and Coach Troy sat me down for what I knew would be the last time before I raced. "Out of all the people I've coached in my entire career, you've been the most up and down, crazy, amazing adventure, and I'm so proud to call you my swimmer. This is the last race of your life, and whether you win or lose you will never ever be replaced in my heart." Coach Troy was a man of few words, and his sentiment touched me to my very core. I started crying, and it went without saying that I felt the same way about him.

As I warmed up, Coach Troy paced me for the last time. Everyone on the team knew this was my last race, and they made a huge deal about every little thing I did that night. "You're never going to warm up at Worlds again!" They were right. I had spent the last 18 years of my life training, the last 12 as a member of the USA National Team, and in a very real way it was the end of an era for me. I didn't know what came next, but I had finally gotten to a place where I could be proud of what was behind me. Normally, before your race, you're in the team area, and the people who are swimming that night wish you good luck and send you off. But that night, for my 400 IM, the entire team came down from the stands at the competition pool and started chanting my name. "Beisel! Beisel! Beisel!" As I walked out to race I was crying, but not because I was frustrated, terrified, or in pain as had been the case so many times. These were tears of sheer joy. That would be the last time I raced with the USA Beisel swim cap I had first earned at the age of 13, and I was overwhelmed with gratitude. The team continued screaming my name, my family cheered from the stands, and I knew that no matter what happened Coach Troy was proud to call me his swimmer. Ironically, I got sixth, just like I had in Rio at the 2016 Olympics. Only this time, I didn't feel like a failure. Finishing the last race of my career, I couldn't help but smile from ear to ear. That day I knew no matter what place I came in, I had won.

CHAPTER TWENTY

I officially retired from professional swimming in December, 2017. I currently lead swim clinics and give motivational speeches all over the country, work closely with USA Swimming, Speedo, and the USA Olympic Committee, and continue to make time to swim, whether that be in a pool or the open water. On January 11, 2016, Li Xuanxu of China, Ye Shiwen's training partner who won bronze in the 2012 London Olympics 400 IM, tested positive for using prohibitive substances (hydrochlorothiazide specifically) following an out-of-competition doping test. She was banned from competition. To this day, whenever I am interviewed, I'm still asked if I think Ye Shiwen was doping when she blasted the 400 IM World Record and beat me. The answer is, I don't know. But there are a lot of things I do know.

I know that despite my best efforts and the amount of time, dedication, and training I put in, that I never achieved what I set out to accomplish. My dream from when I was seven years old, watching the Sydney Olympic Games in my parent's living room, was to win a gold medal. That never happened. Staring at the bright colors, the toned athletes, the explosion of fireworks, and those symbolic interlaced rings, I only saw the glamour and the prestige from the outside looking in. I can tell you, chasing that dream was harder, so much more challenging, demanding, and difficult than I ever could have imagined when I first made up my mind to go for gold. But it was also so much greater in so many ways.

At any point in my training, had you told me my swimming story ended with anything other than a gold medal, I would have been devastated. In fact, I was…many times over. But looking back at my journey, the actuality of following that dream through and doing my utmost to make it a reality molded me into the person I am today. That's not an Olympic gold medalist, and that's okay. Through swimming, I learned commitment, dedication, hard work, leadership, persistence, and resilience. I also realized that it's not always about the outcome and that you can't judge your worth by external factors. And maybe I had to lose to figure that out. Sometimes I look back and think about how much easier things could have been if I hadn't been hell bent on being the best. My life would have been very different, but even knowing the end result, I have no regrets and I wouldn't take back a single moment of my swimming career.

In today's society everyone wants phenomenal things, but they often expect them instantaneously. There's also a rosy view that if you do the right thing and try really hard, everything you want will magically appear. The truth is, if you want to be great at something, it's going to take a lot of time, you're going to fail, and if you truly put yourself out there, eventually you're going to know heartbreak. I guarantee it. But going all out for what you're passionate about is always better than sitting on the sidelines and wondering what you might have been. You can put everything you've got into a goal, and there's no guarantee things are going to turn out the way you want. But what I'm here to tell you is that doesn't mean you failed. Life is crazy and unpredictable and at the end of the day, we've all got two choices. Go fearlessly after what you want, blaze a path, and take a chance, or watch complacently as life happens. The only way to move ahead is to risk failure, and do it again, and again, and again. I never won a gold medal, but the silver lining is what I now know to be certain—if you can find the courage to give your all to what you love, it's impossible to lose.

THE OLYMPIC CREED

The most important thing in the Olympic Games is not to win but to take part, just as the most important thing in life is not the triumph but the struggle. The essential thing is not to have conquered but to have fought well.

– Pierre de Coubertin

ACKNOWLEDGMENTS

Writing *Silver Lining* has been an unbelievably cathartic and gratifying experience. Reflecting on my career not only allowed for years of suppressed memories to resurface, but also revealed to me the incredible number of influential people who guided me throughout my journey. Each of the following individuals played a significant role in my life, and I would be remiss if I did not thank them for their unwavering love and support.

To my parents. Thank you for always believing in me and helping me pursue my crazy, wild dream of becoming an Olympian. Whether you were driving me to swim practice at 5am or buying a plane ticket to watch me compete in the Olympics, you were always there for me. I aspire to be the parents and role models you are one day.

To Danny, the best brother in the world. You are one of the kindest, funniest, most genuine people I know. Thank you for always being the loudest person cheering for me. I hope you realize how proud I am to be your big sister.

To all of my coaches. Every single one of you impacted me in a unique, life-changing way. You are not just coaches; you are friends, mentors, and father figures to me. Behind every great athlete is an even greater coach, and I owe all of my success in the pool to the people who sacrificed much of their lives to make me a better swimmer. Thank you, Josh Laplante, Carl Cederquist, Chuck Batchelor, Gregg Troy, and Matt Delancey, for always guiding me towards my dreams.

To my teammates, who inevitably became my best friends. Thank you for always pushing me to the next level and believing in me, especially when I did not believe in myself. It takes a special type of person to willingly stare at a black line for hours a day, and I attribute our unbreakable bonds to the time we dedicated to our incredible sport.

To my high school best friends, Tara and Heather. You two loved me just as much before the Olympics as you did after. Thank you for always grounding me and pausing your lives to be there for me when I need you most. The three of us make quite the trio.

To Beth. I had no idea the amount of time and perseverance it took to write a book and without you, we would not be where we are now. What started off as a business relationship has blossomed into a beautiful friendship. Thank you for believing in my stories and helping me share my journey with the world.

To my agent, Cejih. You took a chance on me after I retired from the sport and have supported me every day since. You are the first call I make whenever I have a question, and without fail, you always pick up and always have the answer. Thank you for believing in my dreams and helping them continue to spread beyond the pool.

To Nico 11 Publishing & Design team. You took my book without hesitation. I want to thank the incredible group of individuals behind the writing, editing, design, publishing, and photography for *Silver Lining*. Beth Fehr, Marla McKenna, Griffin Mill, Lyda Rose Haerle, Michael King, Michael Nicloy, Chelsey Frost, Kateland Cornine, and Cejih Yung; what was just a collection of stories and memories has turned into an entire book because of your efforts.

To the readers and loyal fans. The countless messages of support I've received throughout my swimming career and beyond has made all of the hard work and sacrifices worth it. I cannot thank each of you enough for your kindness and for investing in my story. I hope to inspire each of you in an impactful and positive way.

To the state of Rhode Island. I couldn't be prouder to represent our small state on a global stage. Having you cheer me on during the most significant moments in my career makes my heart burst with pride. I am and always will be a Rhode Islander.

To the United States of America. I wouldn't want to represent any other country in the world. It has been an honor to compete for the stars and stripes and to continue the legacy of excellence, integrity, and spirit within our Olympic team. Thank you to the men and women who protect and serve our country so athletes like myself can compete in the Olympic Games.

- ELB

Elizabeth Beisel is one of the most well-respected Olympic athletes of the past decade and is widely regarded as the consummate "team leader" among all Olympians. As a three-time Team USA Olympian (2008, 2012, 2016), two-time Olympic medalist and the team captain of the 2016 US Olympic Team, Beisel has had one of the most accomplished and remarkable athletic careers in history.

As impressive as Beisel's athletic accomplishments are, it is her reputation as a team leader, mentor, and motivator that has led to such a loyal following among fans and strong relationships with sponsors. She is an ambassador for the Olympics, Women in Sports, and often speaks to corporations about how to be a team leader. Her perspective spans across three Olympic Games and is easily one of the most unique and sought after views on leadership in the world.

Beisel currently lives in Saunderstown, Rhode Island, where she keeps an active role in advancing women's sports and is a sought-after national speaker. She is involved with organizations focused on sustainability, including Dow Chemical, an Olympic Sponsor, and Save the Bay. In Spring 2019, she was the Keynote Speaker on behalf of Dow Chemical Company at the American Institute of Architects Conference in Las Vegas, Nevada, where she related the importance of sustainability with the Olympic Games. Further, as a Rhode Island native growing up with a close connection to the ocean, Elizabeth has become an advocate for Save the Bay, a nonprofit organization dedicated to improving and protecting Narragansett Bay, located on the northern side of Rhode Island Sound. She is very passionate about ocean sustainability and preserving the world's oceans, and is excited to partner with organizations and events that share similar values.

Beisel's other interests include surfing, hanging at the beach, and traveling to cool new places around the globe!

"I have won plenty of medals and broken plenty of records, but the happiness I experienced when I made my first team in 2008 is second to none. As a little girl, all I ever wanted to do was compete in the Olympics. When that dream finally turned into reality, it was one of the best days of my life."

During the five and a half years I worked with Elizabeth, she directly changed our team culture. Every athlete wanted to hear her stories, work hard with her, and succeed with her. Her kindness, positivity, authenticity, and bodacious personality transforms every room she walks into. I hope each and every one of you get the opportunity to meet Elizabeth one day and experience the incredible individual she is.

- Chuck Batchelor

Made in the USA
San Bernardino, CA
10 February 2020